THE GRAPHIC DESIGN BOOK

SHIRLEY PETERS

SCHOLASTIC INC.
New York Toronto London Auckland Sydney
Mexico City New Delhi Hong Kong

Thank you to my wonderful parents, June and George James, who have encouraged and supported my career in graphic design and illustration; and have kept my every scribble!

ISBN 0-439-26762-5

Published by Scholastic Inc., 555 Broadway, New York, NY 10012, by arrangement with Scholastic Australia Pty Limited.

12 11 10 9 8 7 6 5 4 3 2 1 2 3 4 5/0

Printed in the U.S.A. 08

First American Scholastic printing, December 2000

Typeset in Triplex

Contents

Introduction 4
Layout 5
Lettering 6
Illustration 8
Photography 10
Photomontage 11
Computers 12
Hints and Tips 15
Materials 16

Projects and Posters 17
Spring Fair Poster 18
Colour-In Poster 20
Concert Poster 22
3-D Zoo Poster 24
Garage Sale Poster 26
Canteen Menu Poster 28
School Project Poster 30
School Concert Playbill 32
Wildlife in my Garden 34

Advertising 39
Fruit Shop Mobile 40
Ads for Newspapers and Shop Windows 43
School Fete Newspaper Ad 46

Greeting Cards and Stationery 47
Black Friday Monster Party 48
Pop-out Canary Card 50
Mask Party Invitation 52
Sleep-Over Party Invite 54
Paint your own Cards 56
Stencil your own Cards 57
Design your own Logo 58
Make Copies of your logo 59

Lettering Styles 60

INTRODUCTION

Once, graphic design was called 'commercial art'. It was the art of designing good-looking brochures, magazines, books, advertisements, newspapers, labels and everything that was to be printed. Today, graphic design is still commercial art, plus much more: like designing web pages, CD-ROMs, movie credits and signs.

If graphic design is done well, the product looks good, communication is successful and the audience gets the message. If done badly, communication fails and the message is lost.

This book is a guide to using good design in everything you create. Home work, school fete posters, garage sale posters, even ads for your local shops.

And just for fun, you can design your own logo!

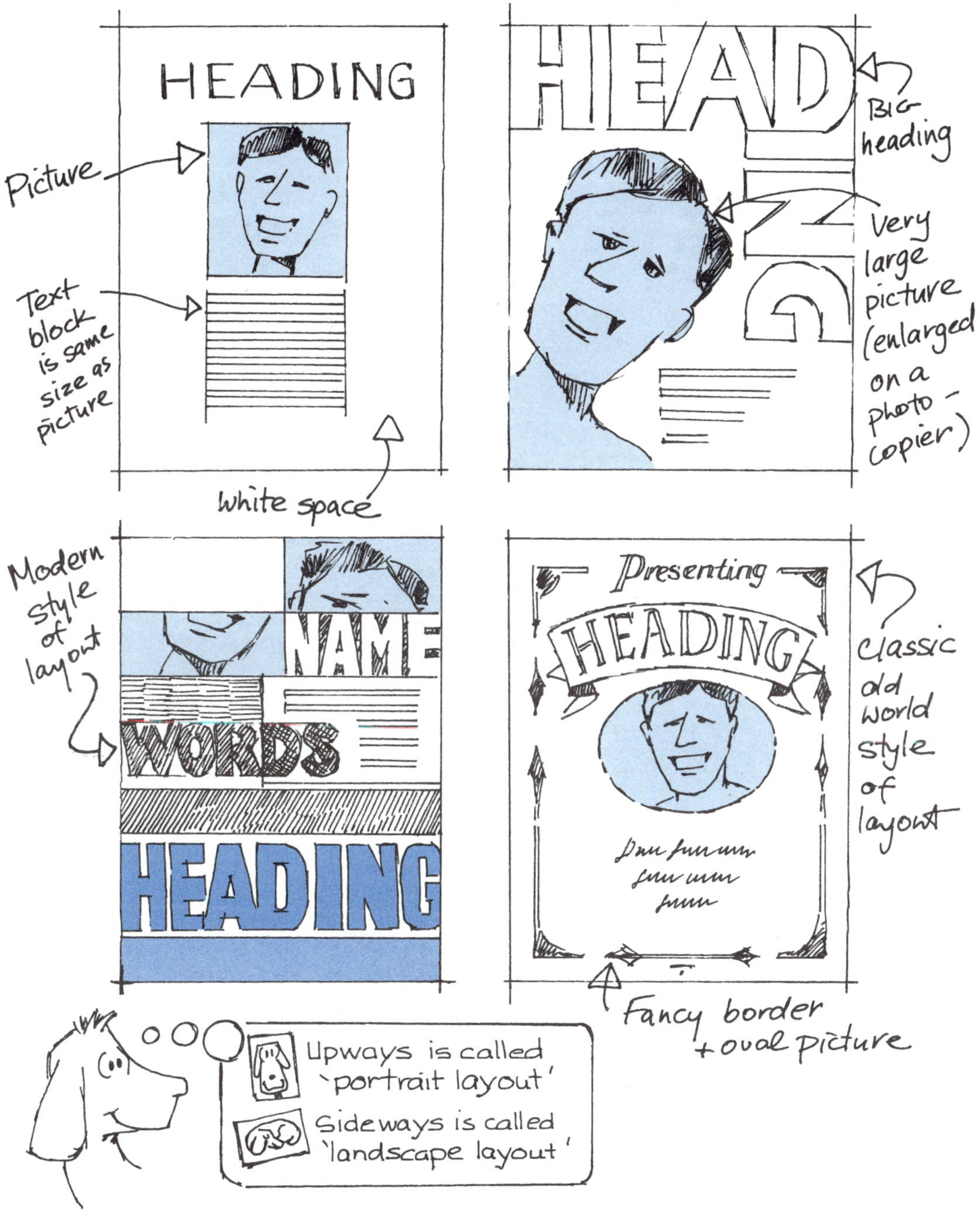

Graphic designers like to sketch a plan of how the job will look when it is finished. This plan is called a 'layout'. It shows how everything is positioned on the page: the heading, the writing, pictures, borders and so on. If there are any problems, like the heading being too large, or there is not enough room for illustrations, then the layout is done again to try and fix the problems.

Always sketch at least one layout before you start. It will help your final design to see different choices.

This layout is how good design begins. Your layout can look interesting or boring. Hopefully it will look great, and when you do the 'finished art' (which means the final version) your efforts will be rewarded with a sophisticated, professional-looking project.

LETTERING

Create your own lettering using this step-by-step guide.

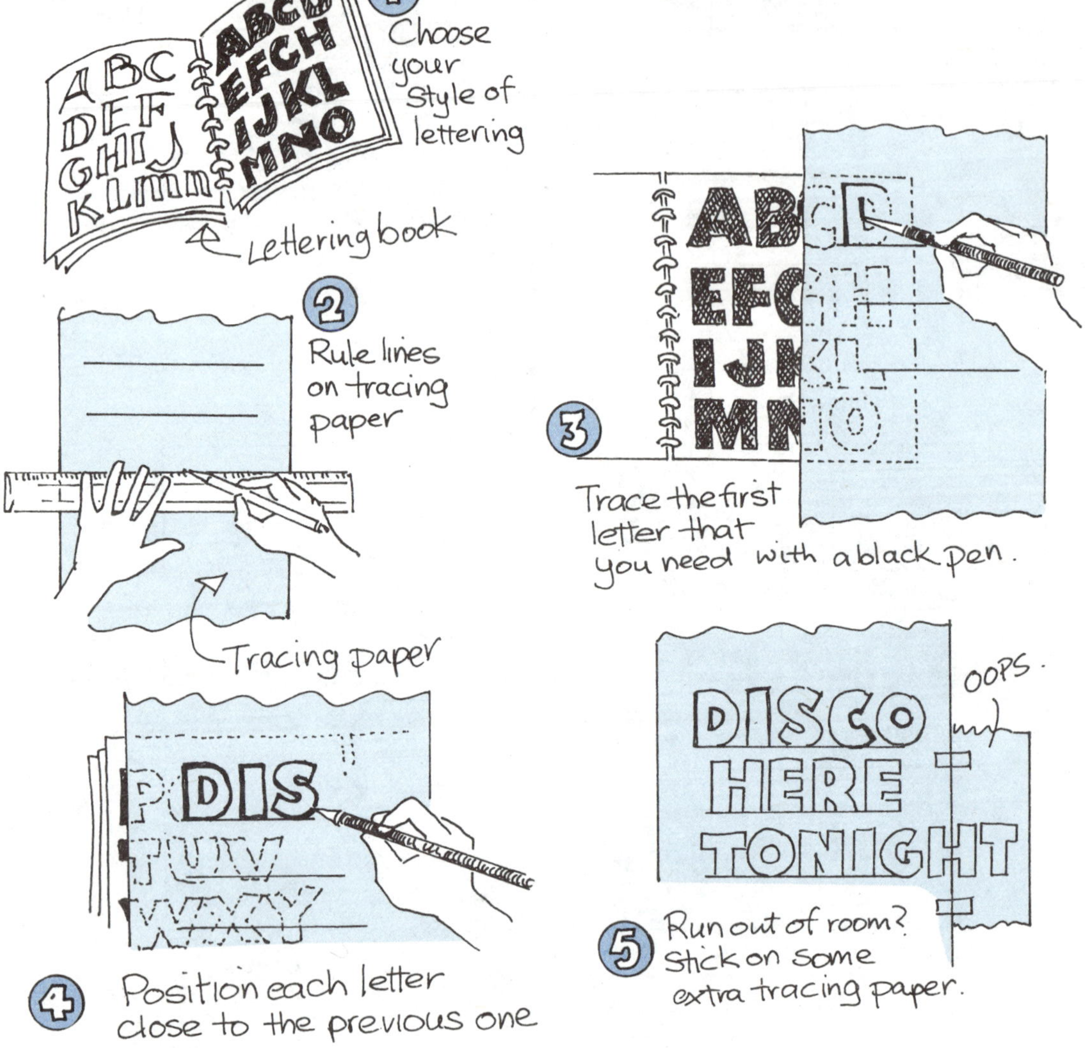

The words in graphic design are the most important element. They deliver the message immediately! Fete. Garage Sale. Art Show. We know what the poster or brochure is about when we read these words.

Choosing the right style of lettering is also very important. Strong bold letters are needed for a rugby poster, and script style letters for an invitation to afternoon tea.

There are many thousands of different styles of lettering. Some are at the back of this book on page 61 or you can copy the everyday examples of lettering in advertisements, in magazines and in newspapers.

If you have a glass top table, put a bright light underneath and shine the light up. You can then trace the letters without getting tired arms.

ILLUSTRATION

We are visual people.
We like to look at pictures. Pictures make communication very easy, and in graphic design we call pictures that we draw illustrations.

You can create new illustrations by copying photographs or drawing the real thing. Either way it will help in your graphic design.

Here are a few useful illustrations that you can use in different jobs. Trace them, or use a photocopier to enlarge them if you prefer.

PHOTOGRAPHY

A modern form of illustration is photography. Use photography in your design to help communicate the message.

HINTS: When taking photos of something small or another person always try to get close. If you are photographing a building you will need to get a long way back. With groups of people, tell them to 'bunch up' and, with animals, give them something to eat so that they stay relatively still.

If you are doing a black-and-white brochure or poster that will be printed or photocopied make sure that the photo has lots of light sections. A photo that is too dark will look like a blob when copied.

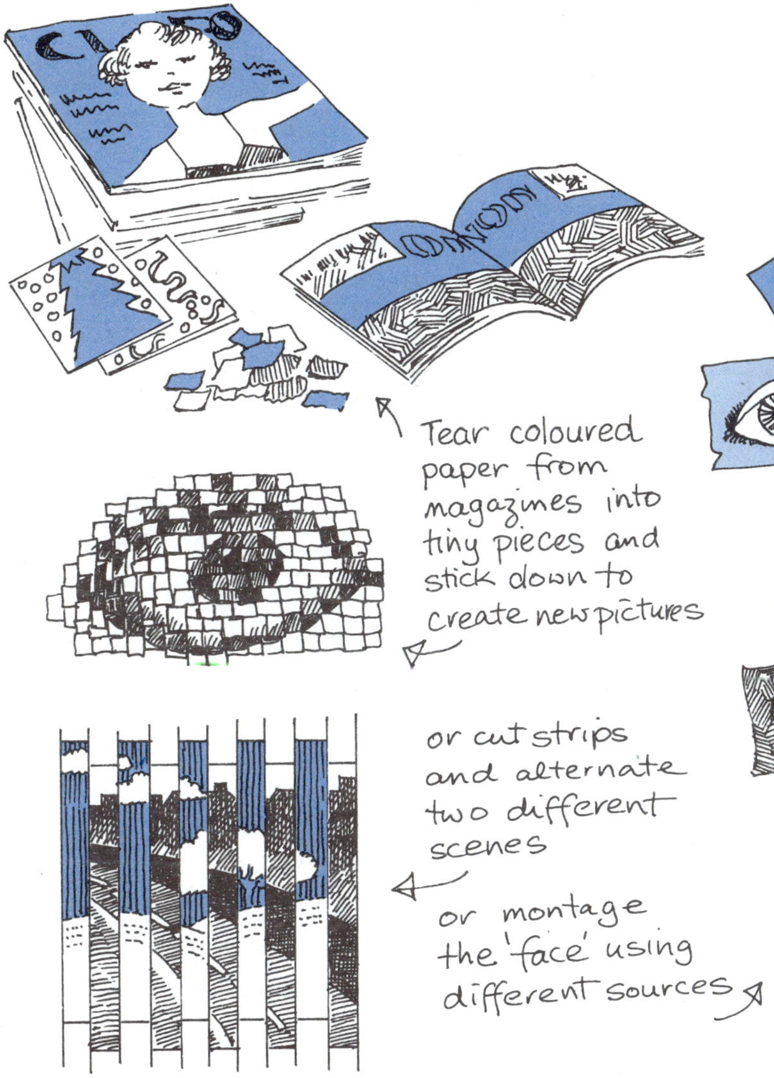

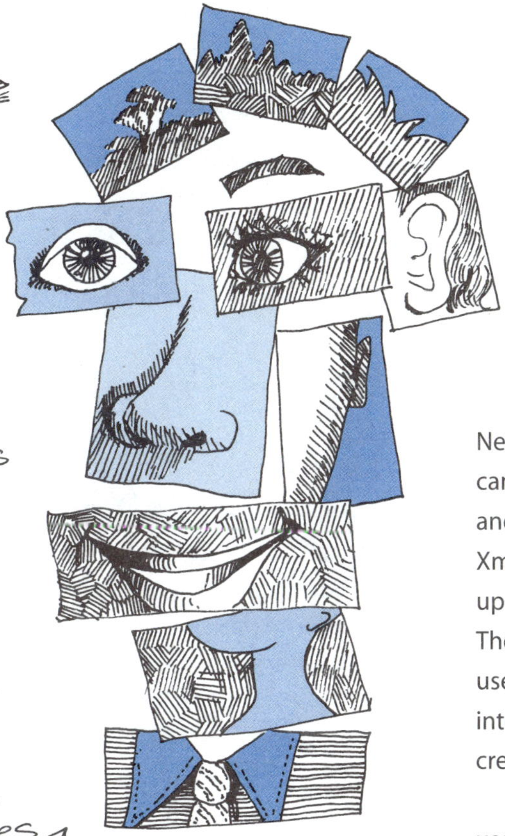

Never throw out used magazines. They can be very useful when illustrating and lettering. Magazines, newspapers, Xmas cards and calendars can be cut up and re-assembled in many ways. They can be torn into tiny pieces and used as a mosaic style picture, or interleaved with another picture to create something entirely new.

Newspaper lettering can be re-used. Just cut the letters out and stick them down; mix styles and sizes for best effects.

COMPUTERS

Computers are used by graphic designers for layouts, lettering and illustration. They are fast, accurate and fun!

If you have a computer at home or at school you will be able to save a lot of time by using it, but beware. It is easy to do bad design on a computer. Do a layout with a pencil and paper first, then follow this design when creating your work on the computer.

To design a brochure or poster on the computer you will need a 'desk-top publishing' program. This enables you to place photographs or illustrations anywhere on the page, and have the text wrap around the pictures.

To draw pictures on your computer you will need a drawing program. You can produce images using just circles, squares and lines.

If you do not have these programs, your plain word processor can do just as well. You can type the words into your computer, make them big, print them out and stick them down onto your 'finished art'.

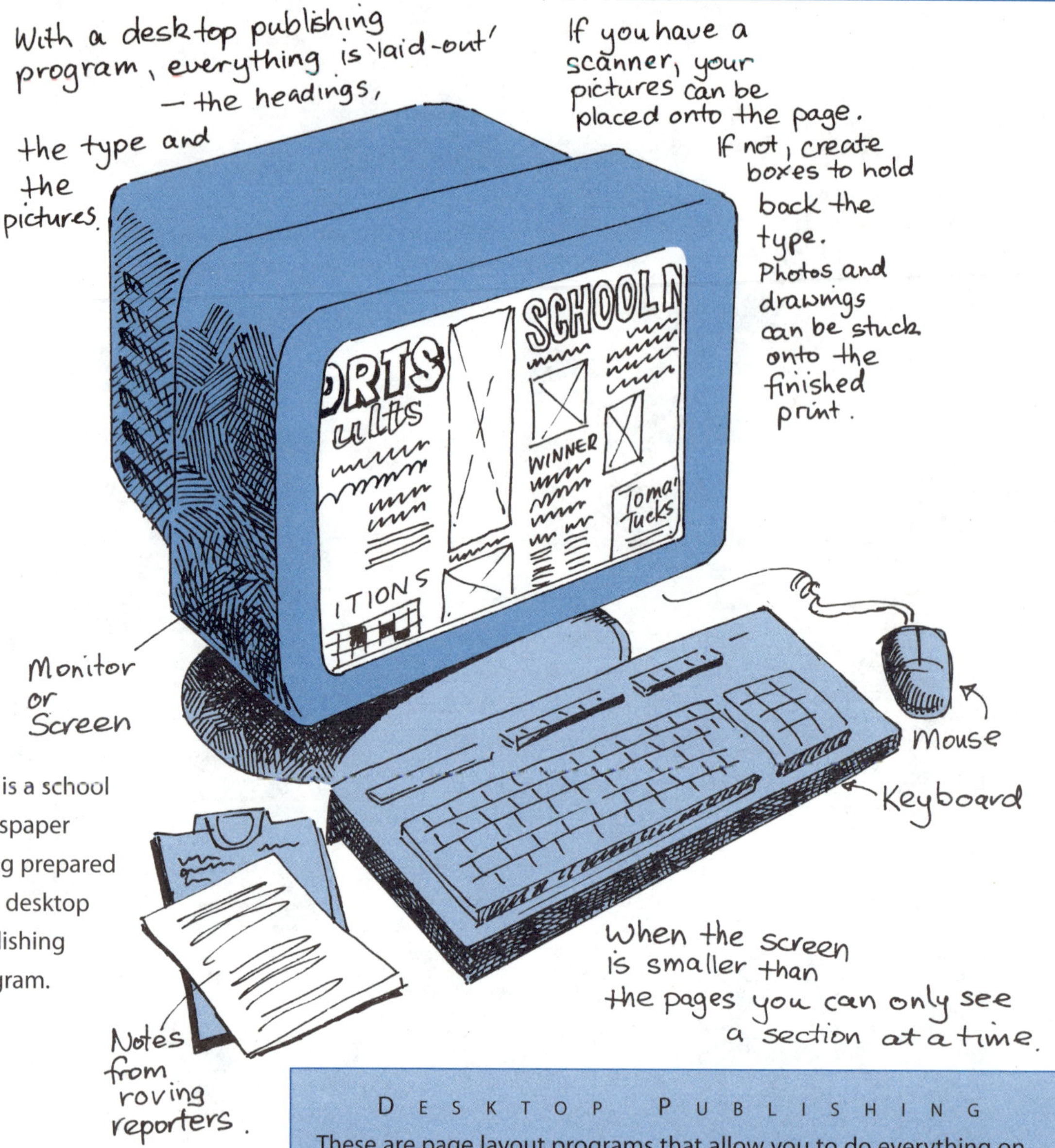

This is a school newspaper being prepared on a desktop publishing program.

DESKTOP PUBLISHING

These are page layout programs that allow you to do everything on the computer screen. They can produce *any* size and style of type, arrange the text in columns or funny shapes, draw basic illustrations and place photographs on the page. They are ideal for newsletters, school magazines and books.

Here are some design words and their meanings.

A **serif** type has lumps on the ends of the letters.

A

A **sans-serif** type has no lumps on the ends of the letters.

A

A **script** type looks like old-fashioned running writing.

Snow

Italic means slanting.

Snow

Bold means thick type.

Snow

Outline is a thin line that goes around the outside of the letters.

Snow

Drop shadow means that the type has a dark area below and on one side of the letters.

Snow

Font is the name of a style of type, eg Helvetica, Times.

This is Helvetica
This is Times

Range left means that the lines of type line up on the left.

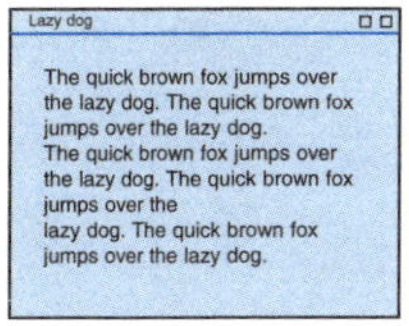

Range right means that the lines of type line up on the right.

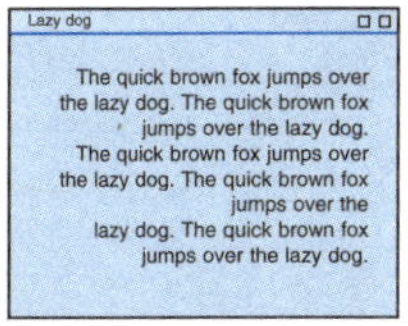

Justified means that they line up both sides.

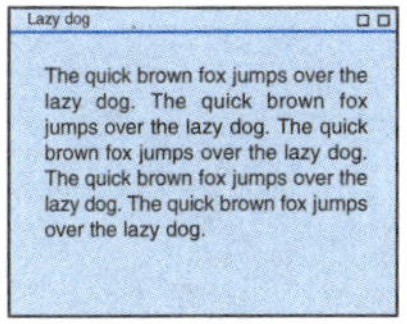

Centred is when the lines are in the middle, not lining up at the sides.

Margins are the space around the outside of the page.

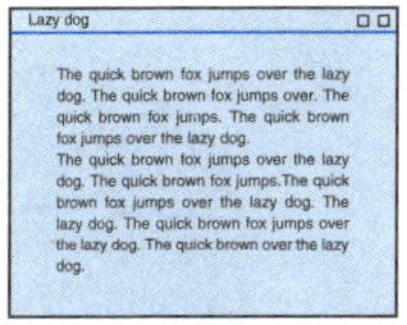

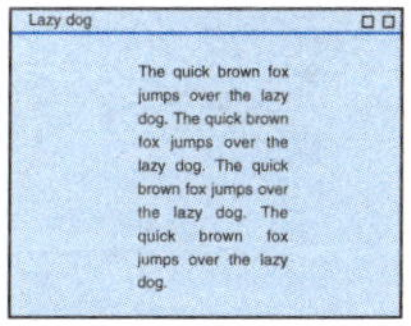

Columns are the vertical rows of type.

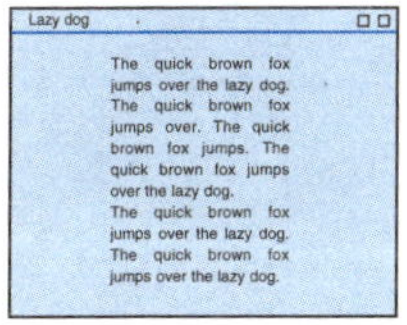

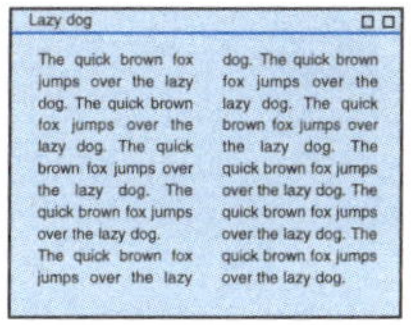

Read the instruction book that came with your program, or ask a teacher or friend to help. You will need to learn how to make all the elements on this page. You will also need to know how to 'edit' type by cutting bits out and pasting them back in. Also, how to check your spelling, and how to 'import' pictures onto your pages.

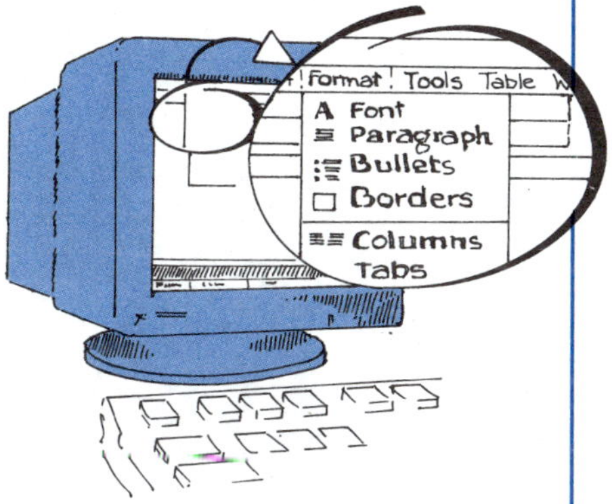

NEWSPAPERS

With a desktop publishing program, a scanner and a printer, you can publish your own newspaper.

P R I N T E R S

Printers enable you to transfer your work from the screen onto paper.

If you do not have a printer, ask at school or your local library. Black and white is best for newspapers and things that have to be photocopied (due to the cost) but colour is best for one-off jobs such as a school project.

T Y P E W R I T E R S

So, you've got a typewriter?

Easy. Start with a layout showing how everything will fit.

Then type your text in one long column, cut it into sections and stick it in place. Draw headings by hand.

Hints and Tips

Here are a few general pointers for you to remember as you create your own graphic design.

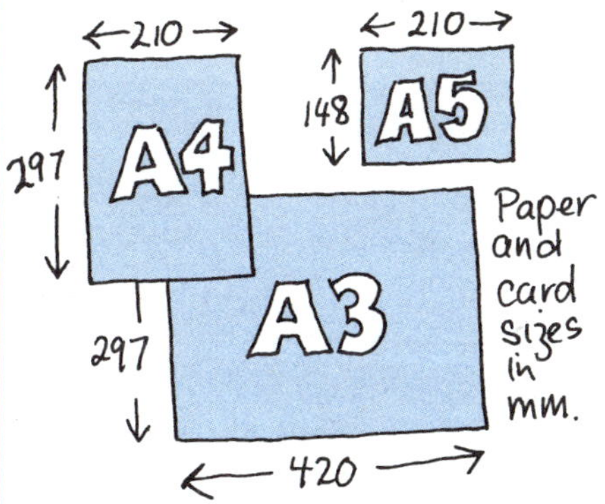

These are the basic sizes of paper and cardboard:

A5 210 x 148 mm

A4 210 x 297 mm

A3 420 x 297 mm

A5 is half of A4, which is half of A3, which is half of A2 etc.

Take care not to crumple your paper when using a glue stick. Hold the paper steady, and wipe from the centre to the edge.

When photocopying pages that have cut-out sections, you will get a grey 'shadow' on the cut edges. This needs to be painted with white out, and then re-photocopied.

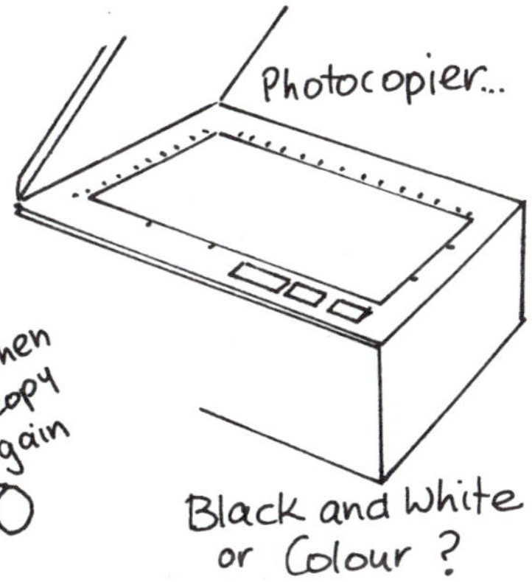

All photocopying in this book is black and white, as this is the cheapest and most 'available' method of reproducing your pages.

If you have access to a colour photocopier, try using coloured background papers and coloured pens in your projects.

HOW TO FOLD CARDBOARD

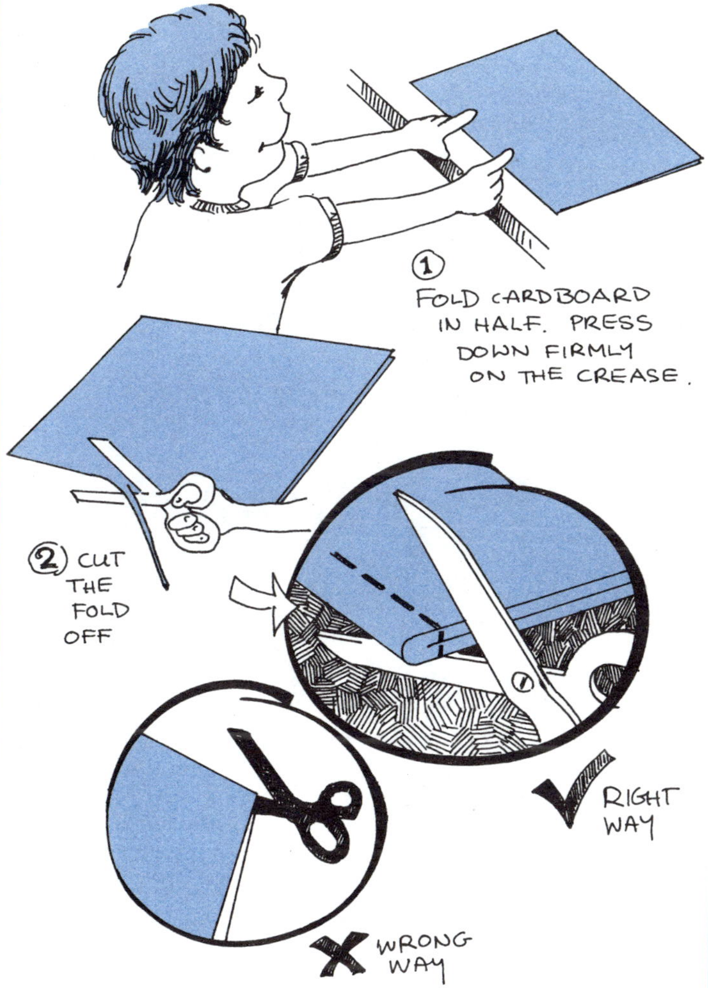

Materials

You will need a desk, chair and some basic art materials.

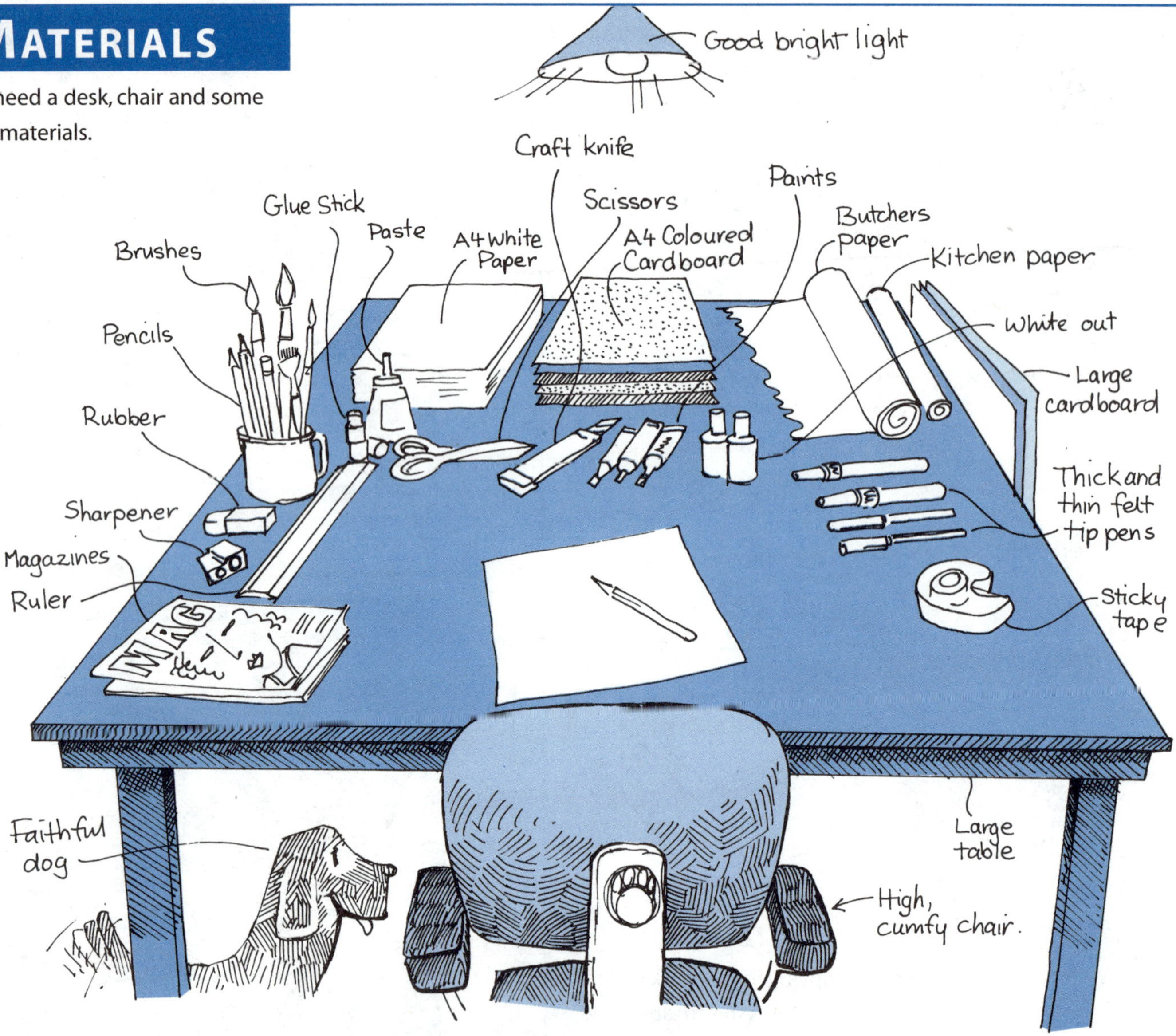

HINT: Keep a copy of everything that you create. This collection of your work is called a 'portfolio' and shows people how clever you are! And one day it might help you get a job as a graphic designer.

PROJECTS & POSTERS

In this section there are many different projects for you to use. On the left of each double-page spread there is a 'photocopy master' of the finished project which you can copy or trace, after making the necessary changes. On the right there are step-by-step instructions if you would rather start from the beginning. Using either method you might need to follow the **handlettering** instructions on pages 6 and 7. And some **lettering styles** for you to trace start on page 61.

How to use the 'Photocopy Master'

Start with a photocopy of the poster.

White out the parts that you want to change

Stick on the new parts, then photocopy again.

School's Name
SPRING
FAIR
Saturday
15th October
10am - 4pm 68 View St. Argle

SPRING FAIR POSTER

Here is a simple school poster that will start you off with cutting, pasting and handlettering.

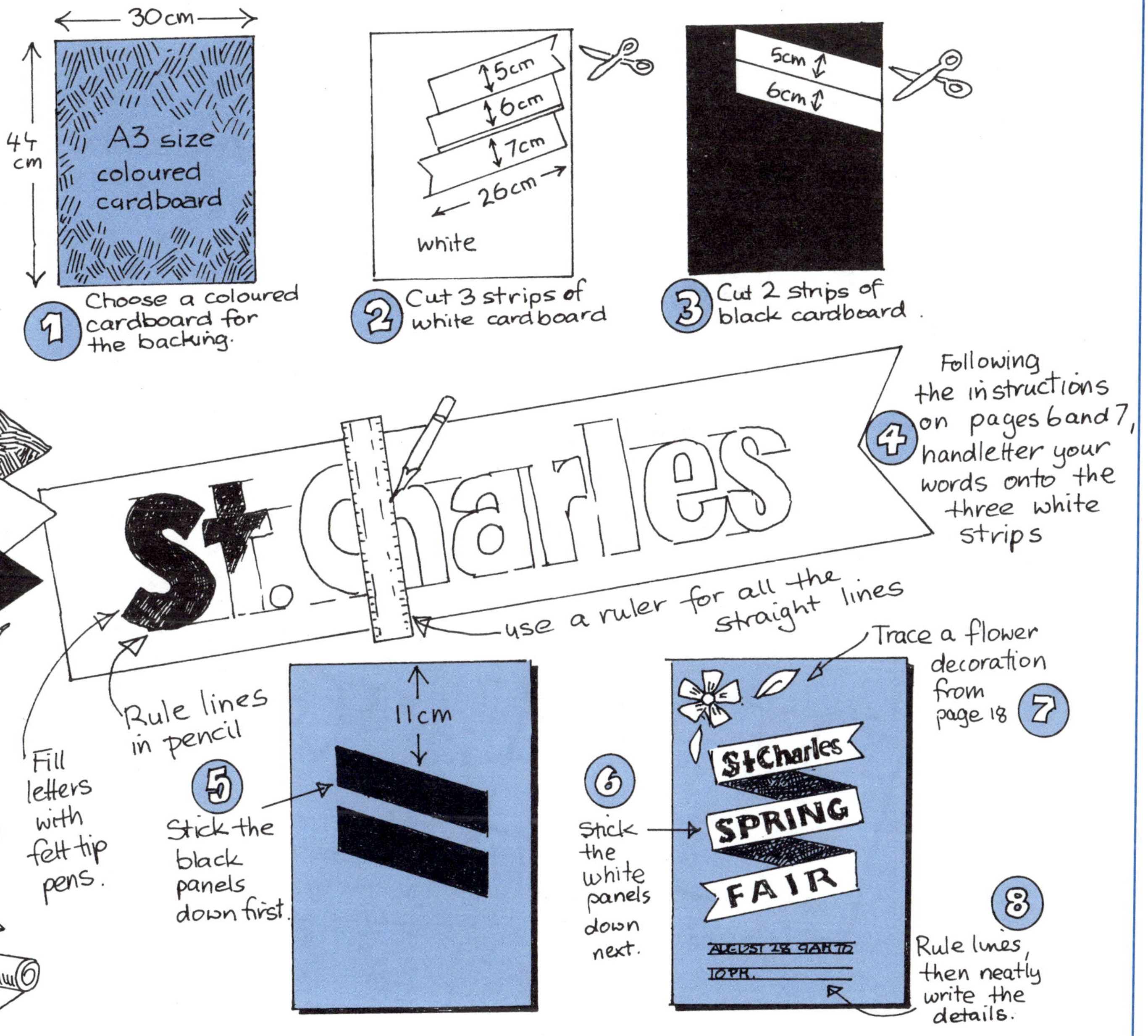

YOU'LL NEED . . .

- A3 sheet bright coloured cardboard
- A4 sheet white cardboard
- A4 sheet black cardboard
- Pencil & rubber
- Thick black felt tip pen
- Thin black felt tip pen
- Scissors
- Ruler
- Tracing paper (same as kitchen paper)
- Glue stick
- White out

ANYTOWN SCHOOL
FETE
SATURDAY
23rd SEPT
10am – 3pm
HOT DOGS
HAMBURGERS
SLIDES 'N' RIDES
BOTTLE TOMBOLA
POT PLANTS
HOMEMADE JAMS
JUMPING CASTLE

COLOUR -IN POSTER

This poster is designed to be photocopied and then coloured with pencil or paints. You could ask the kids at school to colour one each, then stick it up in their favourite shop.

YOU'LL NEED . . .

- A4 sheet white cardboard
- A4 sheet thick white paper (cartridge)
- A4 paper
- Pencil & rubber
- Tracing paper
- Ruler
- Thick and thin black felt tip pens
- Scissors
- Glue
- White out

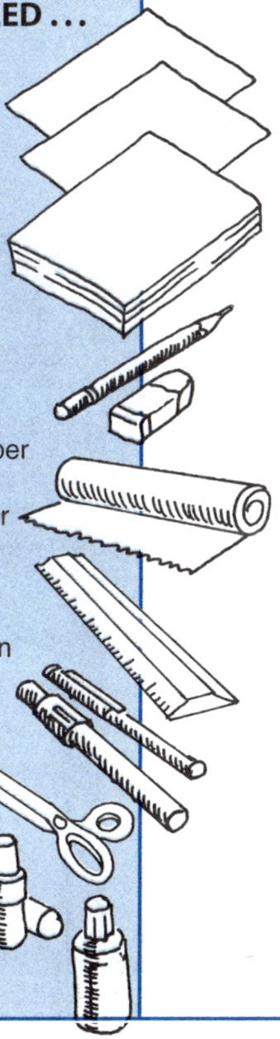

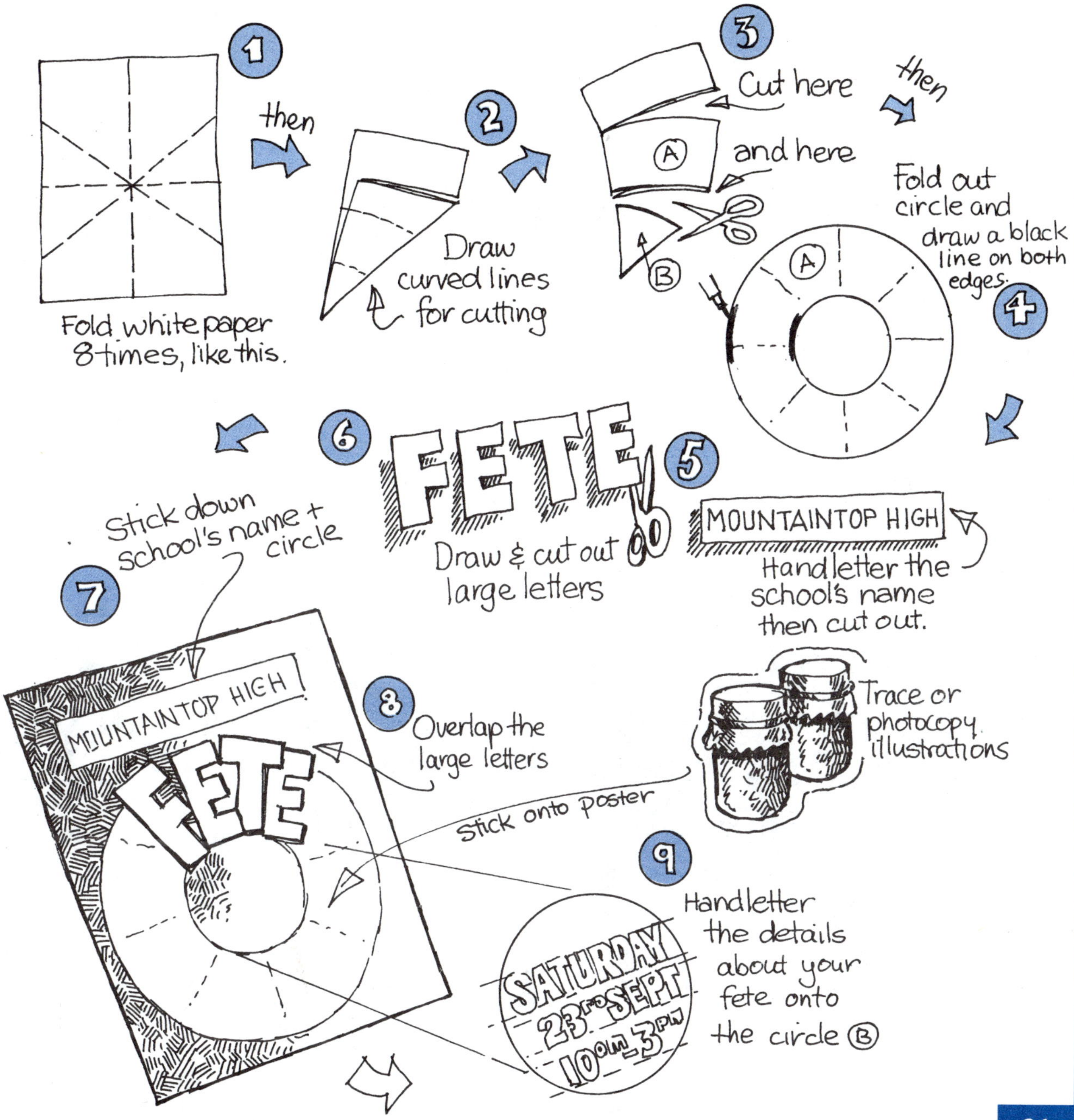

CONCERT
JAZZ • MOOG • SWING
Swing and jive to this
exciting, lively performance
by the award winning
BRASSIMO Band.
Just back from their
successful US Tour,
Brassimo will treat us to their
special show that brought the
house down at Carnegie Hall!
Don't miss this special event.
One night only! Seats are
limited, so BOOK NOW!
Ph: 08 9900 0000
GUMTREES CONCERT ROOM
144 EUCAL HIGHWAY
WATERSVALE
5TH MAY 8PM
BRASSIMO

CONCERT POSTER

This poster uses white lettering on a black background. This is called reverse lettering.

Cut the letters out in groups of three or four, rather than individually.

Use computer type if you prefer.

YOU'LL NEED . . .

- 18 cm x 21 cm sheet white cardboard
- 6.5 cm x 21 cm sheet black paper
- A4 paper
- Pencil & rubber
- Tracing paper
- Ruler
- Thick and thin black felt pens
- Scissors
- Glue
- White out

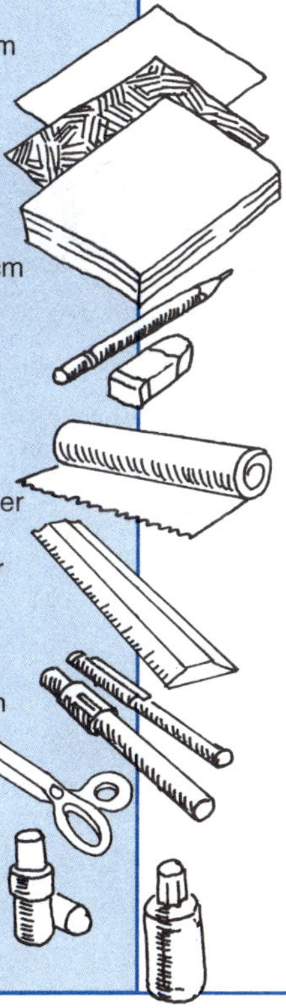

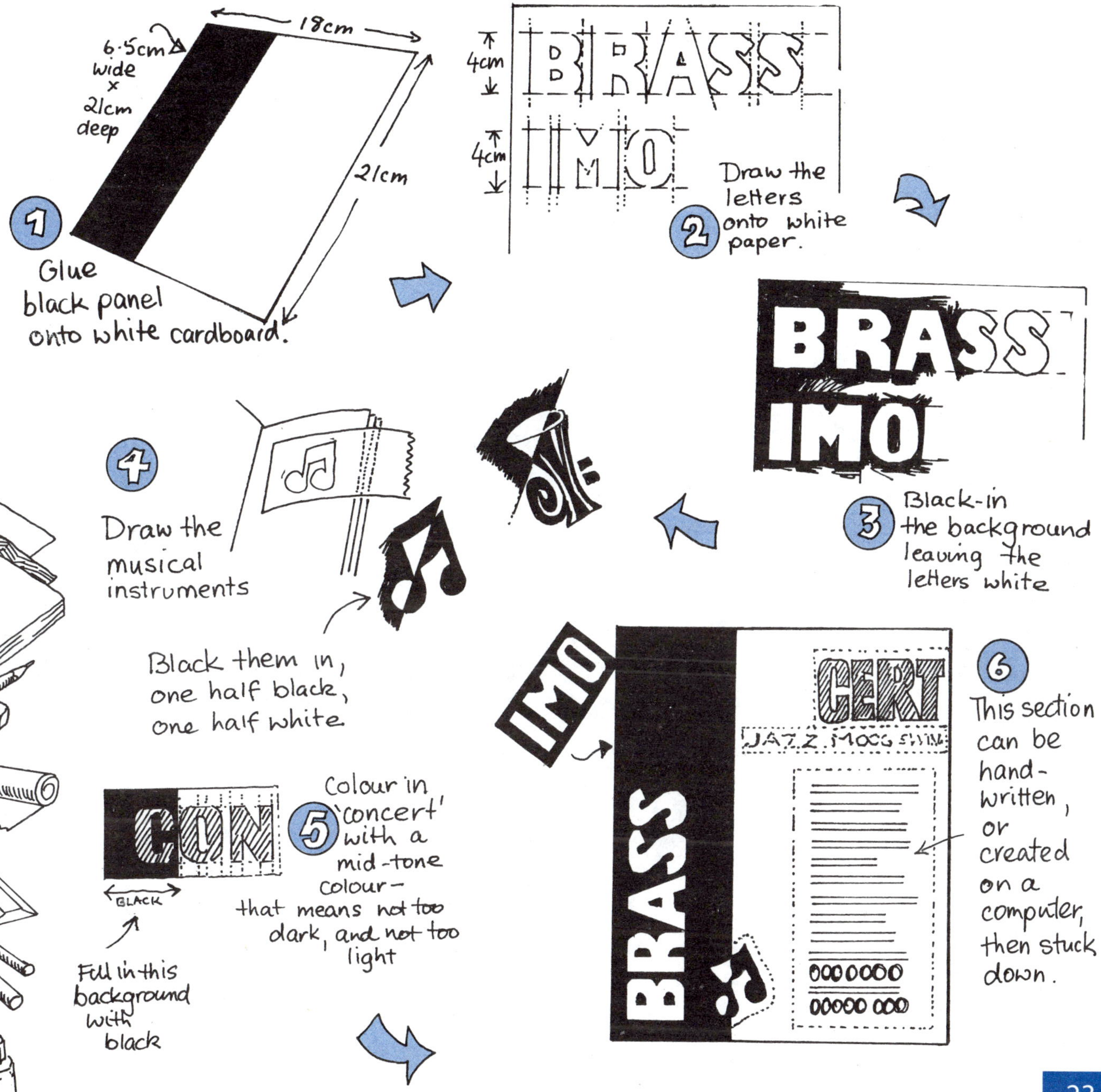

VISIT YOUR
ZOO
OPEN
7am to
6pm
$10
for kids

3-D ZOO POSTER

This poster has special panels that sit out from the background cardboard.

They are attached with 'z' hinges and wriggle in the wind!

Not for photocopying, although it might look very interesting if you do!

YOU'LL NEED . . .

Three or four A4 sheets of coloured cardboard

White A4 paper

Pencil & rubber

Tracing paper

Ruler

Thick and thin black felt tip pens

Scissors

Glue

White out

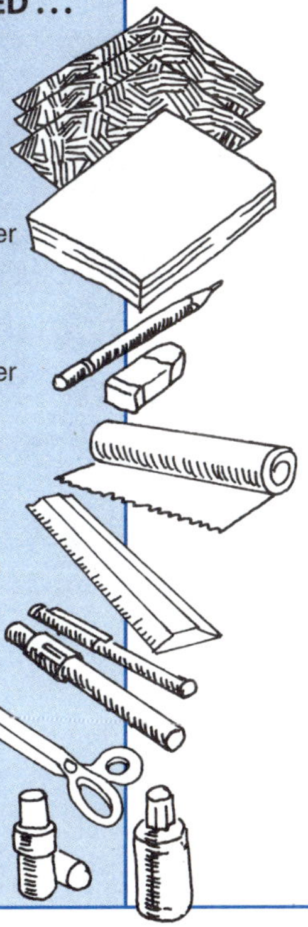

GARAGE SALE

PLUS
____
____
____
____
____
____

SATURDAY 14 • 10am

123 Main Street, Uptown

GARAGE SALE POSTER

This is a useful poster that is easy to see from a distance, therefore it is good to put on telegraph poles. Photocopy the 'master' and make it yours by changing the details, or start from the beginning with these instructions.

YOU'LL NEED . . .

- A4 sheet of cardboard
- A4 paper for illustrations
- Tracing paper
- Pencil & rubber
- Ruler
- Thick and thin black felt tip pens
- Scissors
- Glue
- White out

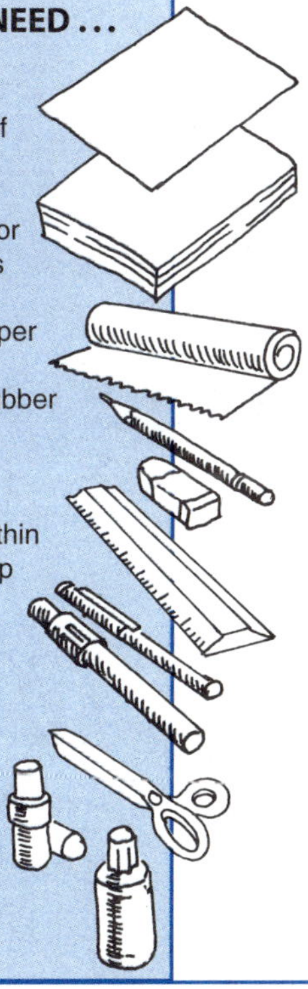

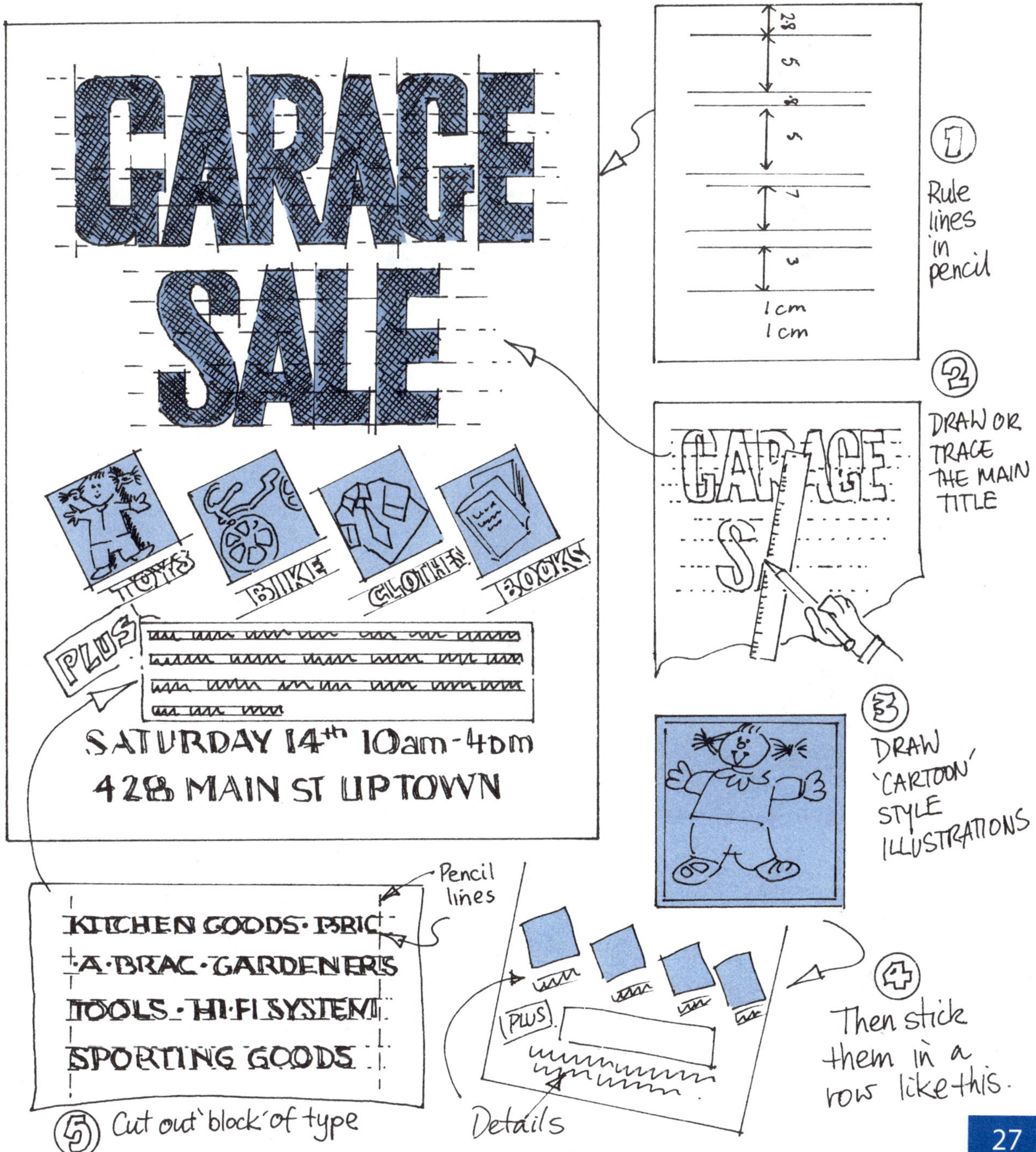

CANTEEN
MENU
RECESS
HOT FOOD
SWEETS
SANGERS
DRINKS
FRUIT
EXTRAS

CANTEEN MENU POSTER

This poster is made from cut-out letters and photographs of food stuck onto the backing board. The menu list can be handwritten, with little photos glued on. Cut out the list, and glue it onto the cardboard.

YOU'LL NEED . . .

- A4 sheet of cardboard
- A4 paper for menu list
- Black cardboard
- Magazines & newspapers
- Pencil & rubber
- Ruler
- Thick and thin black felt tip pens
- Scissors
- Glue
- White out

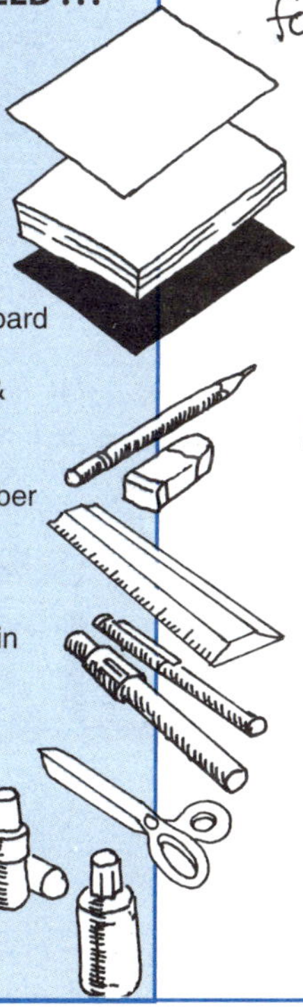

CAROLINE CHISHOLM

ELIZABETH MACARTHUR

4 FAMOUS WOMEN OF HISTORY

FLORENCE NIGHTINGALE

MOTHER TERESA

SCHOOL PROJECT POSTER

This poster is about famous women, but you could do something else. For example: Four Favourite Book Characters or Four Extinct Dinosaurs.

YOU'LL NEED . . .

- A4 sheet of cardboard
- A4 paper for illustrations and title
- A4 black paper
- Pencil & rubber
- Ruler
- Thick and thin black felt tip pens
- Scissors
- Glue
- White out

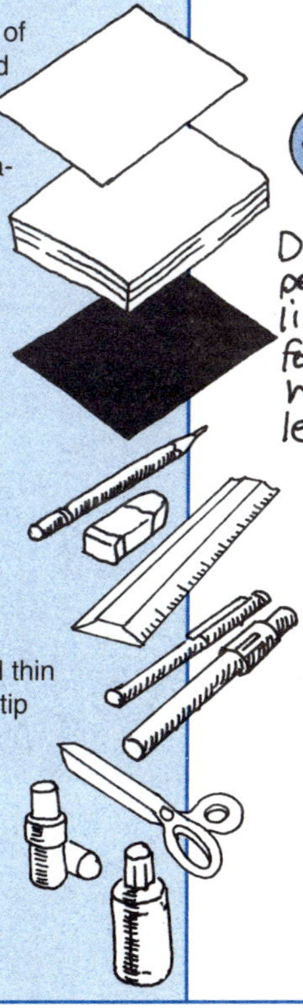

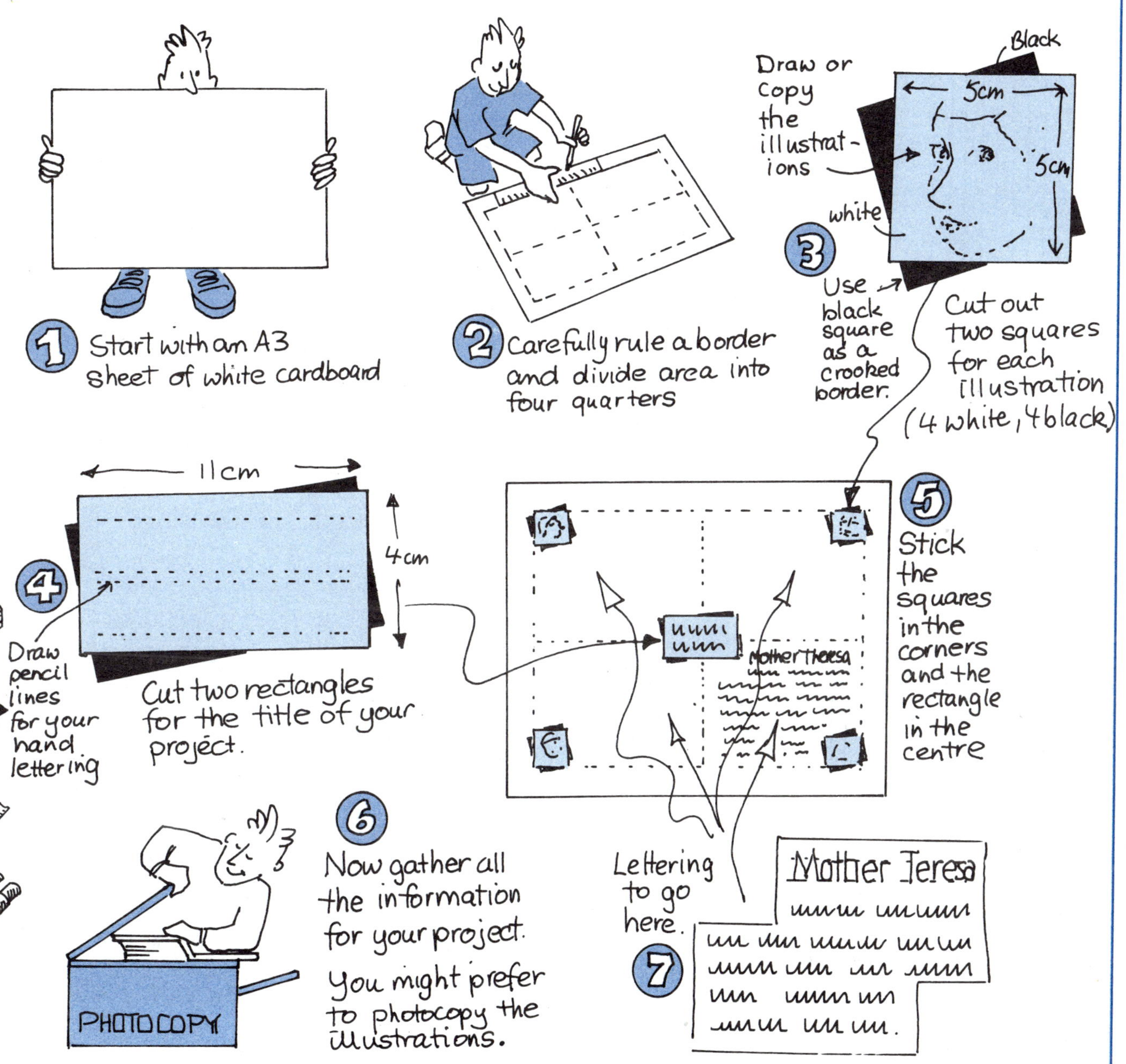

FOLD
WEST TOWN SCHOOL PRESENTS...
FRACTURED
FAIRY
TALES
WITH THANKS TO
OUR SPONSORS
LEO'S
MEATS
THE BEST BUTCHER
IN TOWN
PH. 98091113
PUTNEY
FLOWER
SHOP
for beautiful bouquets
Ph 9809 33332
JP's
the PIZZA PARLOUR
BEST FOOD $
SERVICE
ACT ONE
ACT TWO
ACT THREE
THE STARS

SCHOOL CONCERT PLAYBILL

A playbill is a brochure that tells the audience about a play that they are watching. It lists the 'acts' and the cast of characters.

This playbill is made by folding an A4 paper.

This is how a 'folded brochure' is created from one A4 paper.

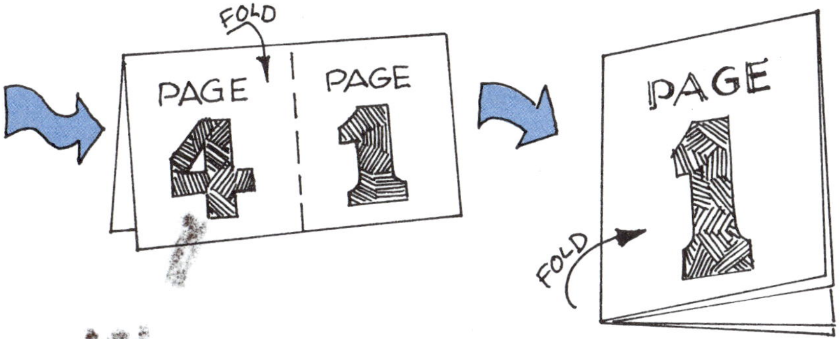

YOU'LL NEED . . .

A4 sheet of paper

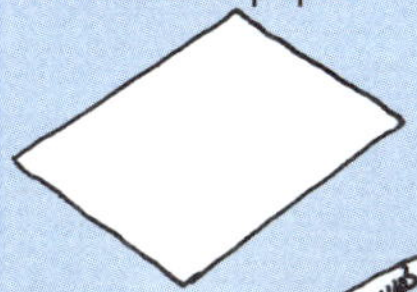

Pencil & rubber

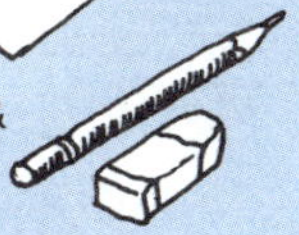

Ruler

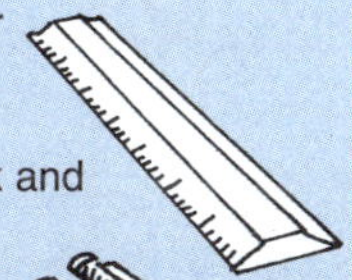

Thick and thin black felt tip pens

Scissors

Glue

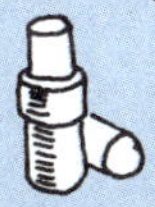

White out

1. Start by folding your A4 page into quarters. Mark each page with its number (in pencil) then fold the page out flat.

2. Use hand-lettering or a computer for each page, add stars and clouds from page 57.

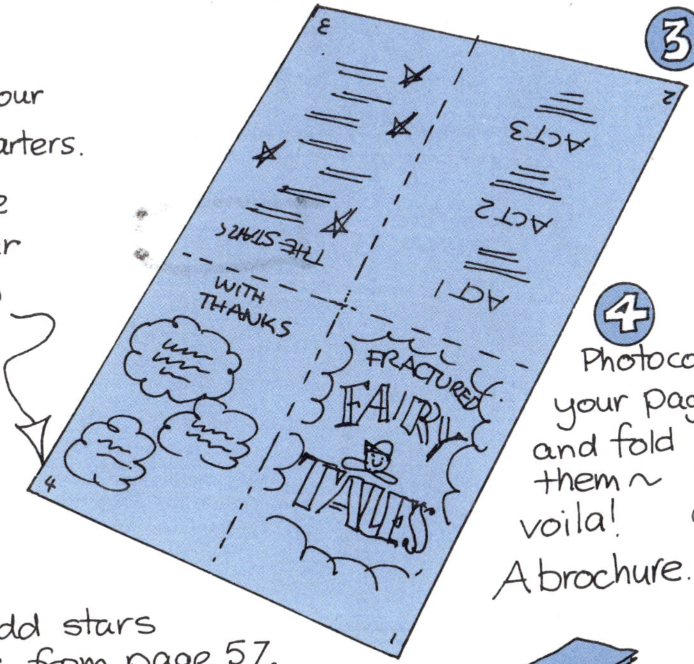

3. Pages 2 and 3 must be upside down.

4. Photocopy your pages and fold them ~ voila! A brochure.

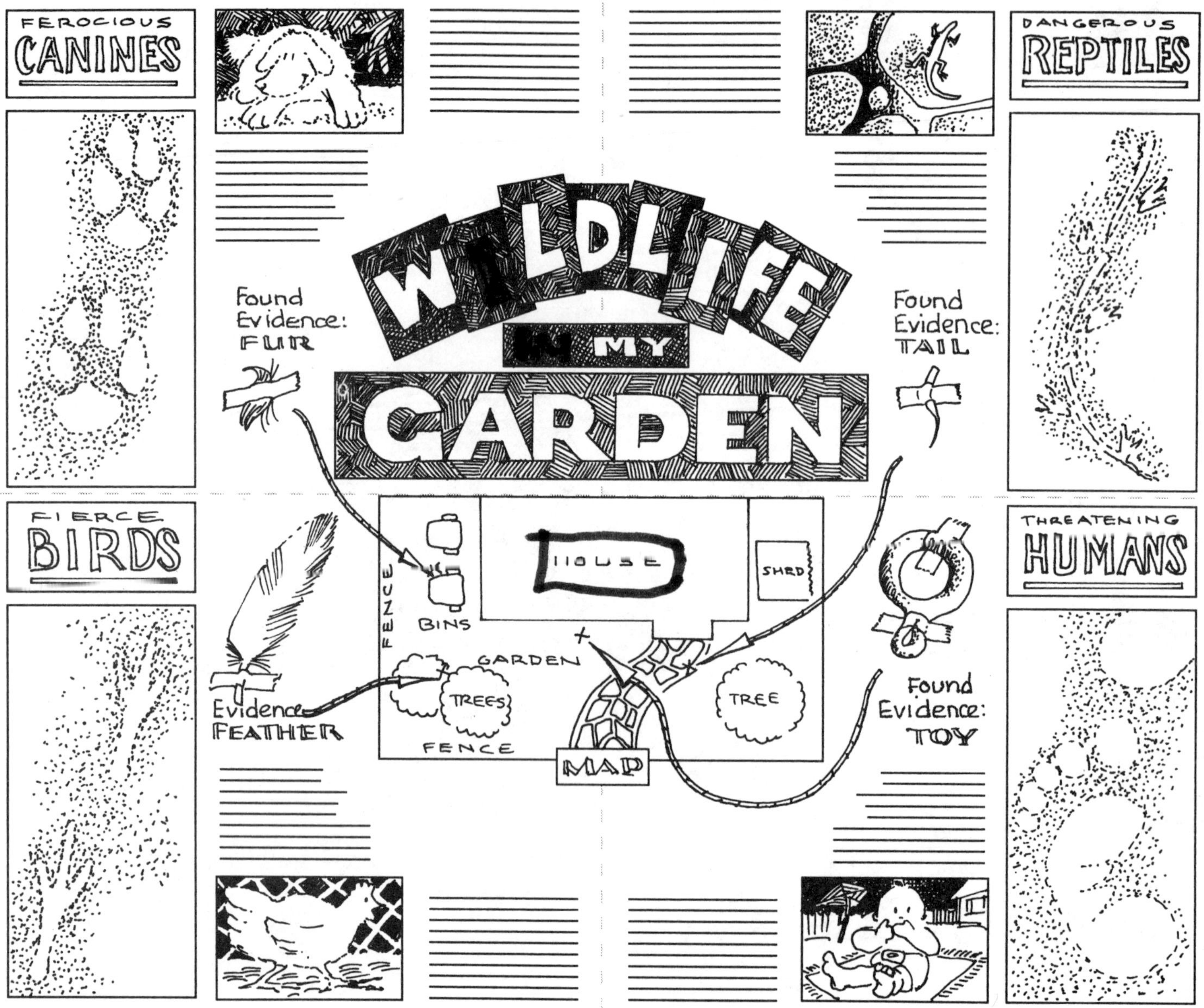
FEROCIOUS
CANINES
DANGEROUS
REPTILES
WILDLIFE
IN MY
GARDEN
Found Evidence: FUR
Found Evidence: TAIL
FIERCE
BIRDS
THREATENING
HUMANS
FENCE
BINS
HOUSE
SHED
GARDEN
TREES
TREE
FENCE
MAP
Evidence: FEATHER
Found Evidence: TOY

WILDLIFE IN MY GARDEN

Here is a school project that uses footprints and real things from your garden. It also involves photography and map drawing.

FOR FOOTPRINTS YOU'LL NEED . . .

4 sheets of newspaper

A bucket of fine sand

4 x A4 sheets of coloured paper

Glue

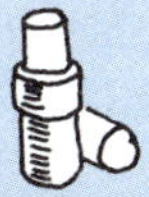

1. Start this project by looking for birds and animals in your garden. The bigger ones will leave footprints in wet sand, so . . .

2. Put newspaper on the ground near places where animals are likely to tread. Spread wet sand on the paper. Leave overnight.

3. Cover a piece of coloured paper with glue.

4. Press paper (with the glue side down) onto the sand prints.

5. Pull up the sheet and VOILA! Your prints are ready to add to your project.

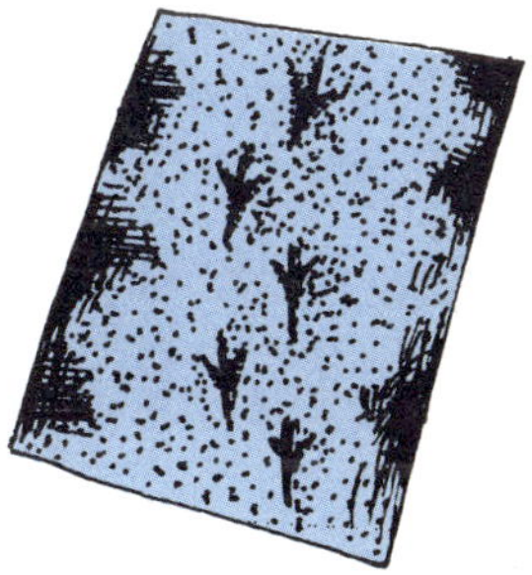

WILDLIFE IN MY GARDEN

6. Take photos of the animals in the day. (Or draw the animal, or get pics from a magazine.)

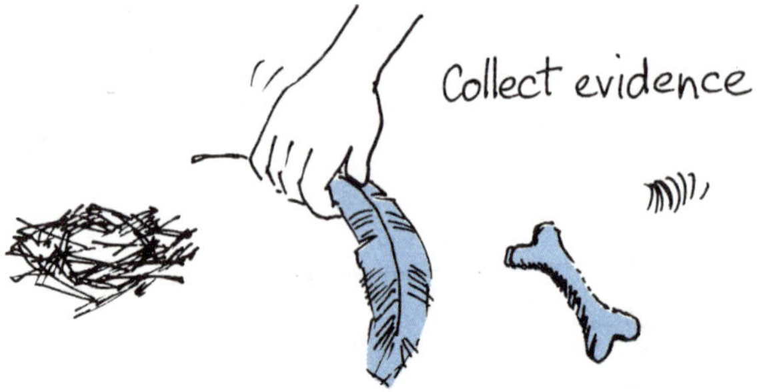

7. Look very carefully for other evidence of their being in your backyard, veranda or park. (No poos, thank you.)

8. Draw a map of the area. Place a cross where each piece of evidence or footprint was found.

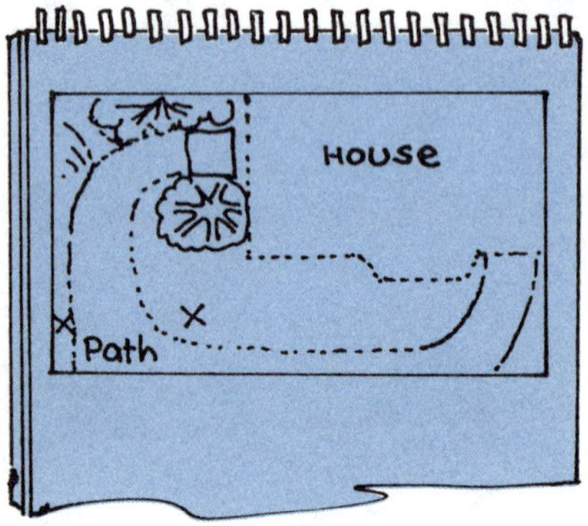

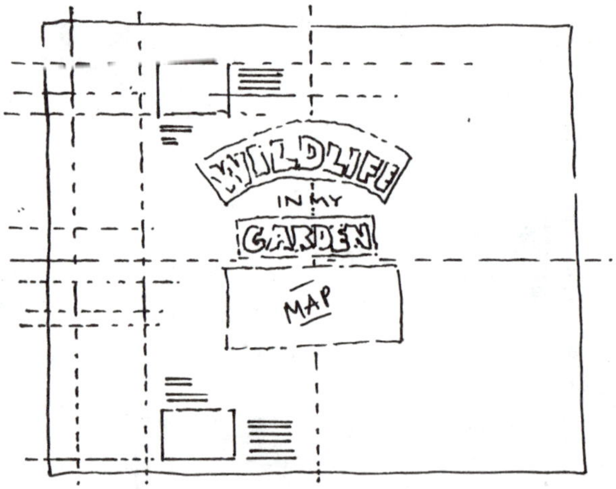

9. Now that you have gathered all the elements for your project, you will need to create a layout on paper.
Start by dividing the page into quarters. Sketch the heading and the map in the middle. Put the animals in one quarter each. This will show you how the elements will fit on the board.

WILDLIFE IN MY GARDEN

FOR THE REST YOU'LL NEED . . .

A camera

Sketch pad or paper

Very large paper for the layout

Large cardboard

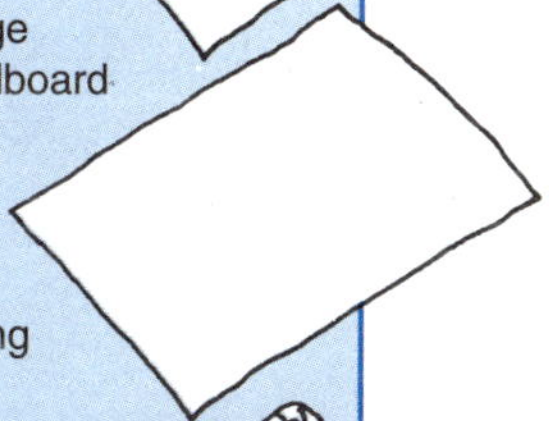

String

Pencil & rubber

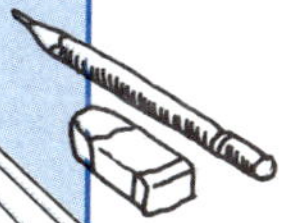

Ruler

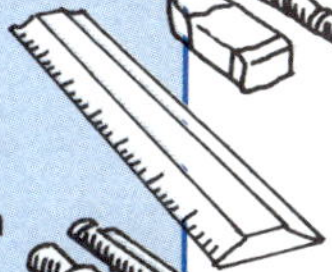

Thick and thin black felt tip pens

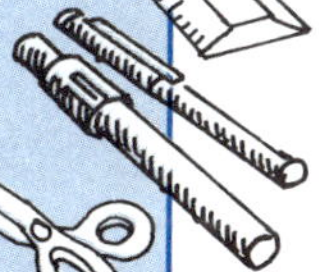

Scissors

Glue

White out

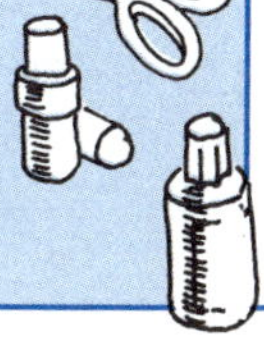

Handlettering

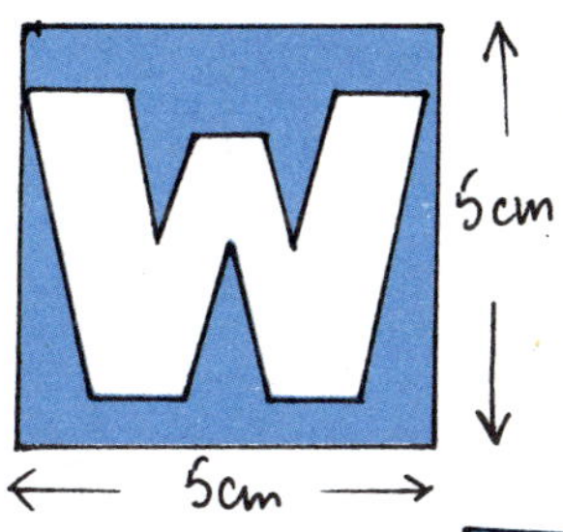

10. Trace or draw your letters onto squares of paper.

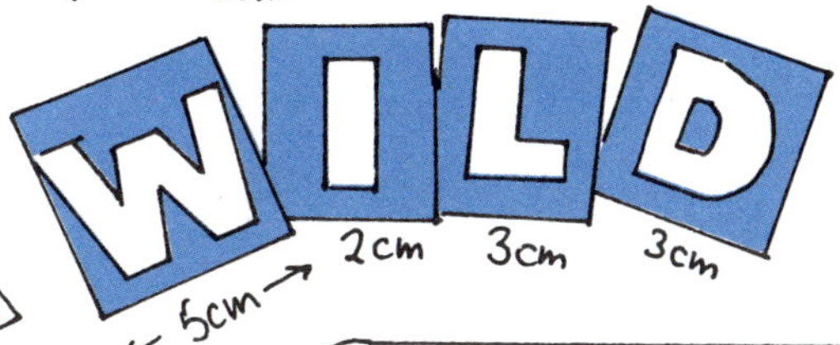

Hint:

Make the letters the same height – about 5cm – but vary the width to match the letters eg. 'W' is twice as wide as 'I'.

Handwritten Text

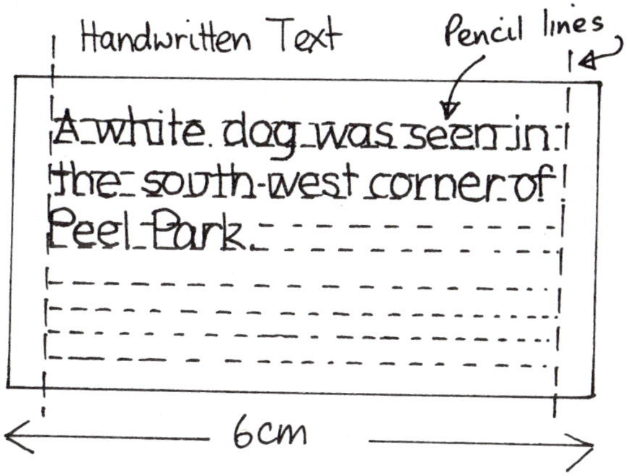

Computer Text

11. If you can type the smaller text on a computer or typewriter, the finished project will look more professional.

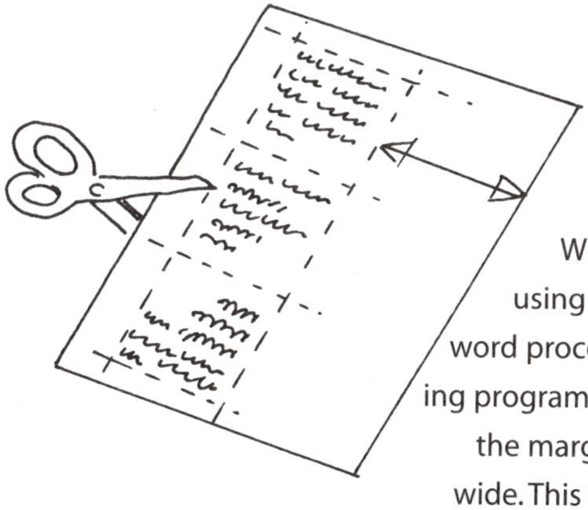

When using the word processing program set the margins wide. This will make the text narrow.

Attaching stuff

12. Poke the ends of the string through holes in the card.

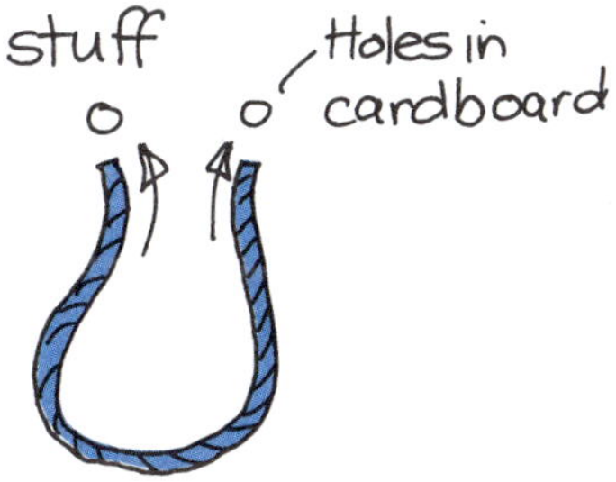

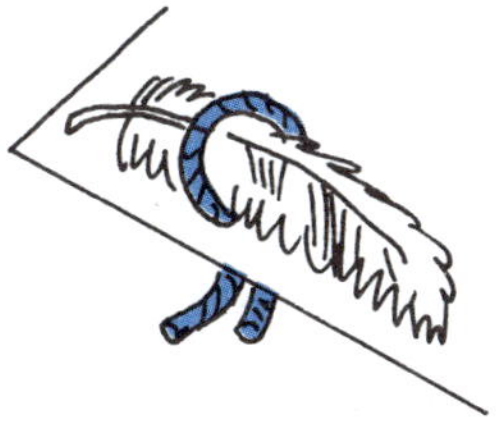

13. Pull ends tight while placing object under loop. Tie at back.

WILDLIFE IN MY GARDEN

14. Assemble all the elements onto the cardboard, using glue for paper and string for the objects.

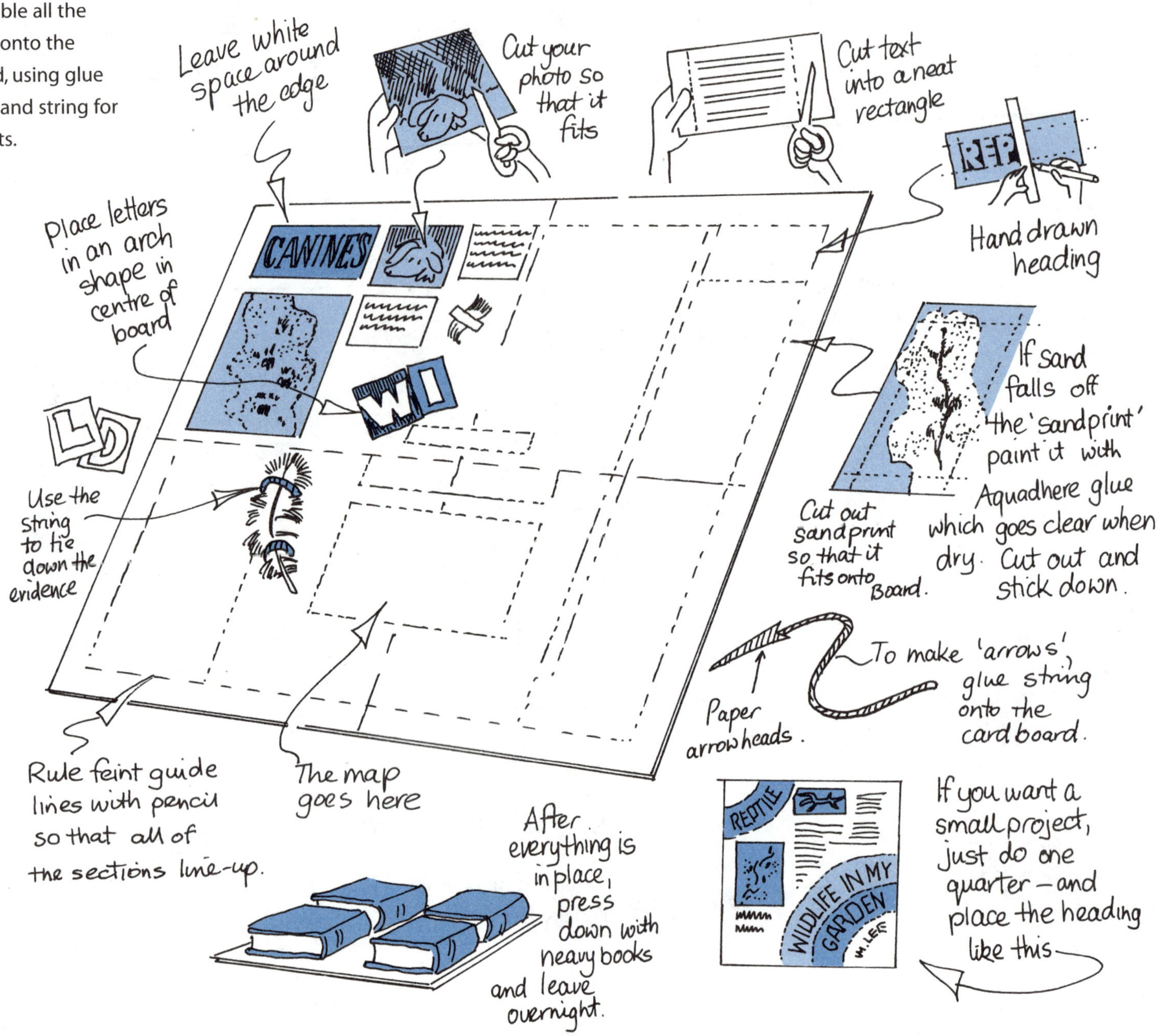

ADVERTISING

We often want to sell things. Creating an ad and placing it in a shop window is an easy and effective way to reach potential customers. You might also be able to advertise in a local newspaper, although this is usually very expensive. Either way, good layout is important so that your ad looks attractive. Posters which hang in stores are called 'point-of-sale' and you can create a fun three-dimensional poster for your local shop.

A HANGING MOBILE will swing slowly in the breeze. Make one for the local fruit shop . . .

and one for your baby sister's bedroom.

FRUIT SHOP MOBILE

This mobile has four sides and turns slowly in the breeze. Covered with bright colourful pictures, it looks great and will attract heaps of shoppers.

YOU'LL NEED . . .

- 4 large sheets of heavyweight coloured cardboard (54 x 45 cm)
- Scissors
- Long ruler
- Hole punch
- Stapler
- String
- Pencil & rubber
- Thick and thin black felt tip pens
- Glue
- White out

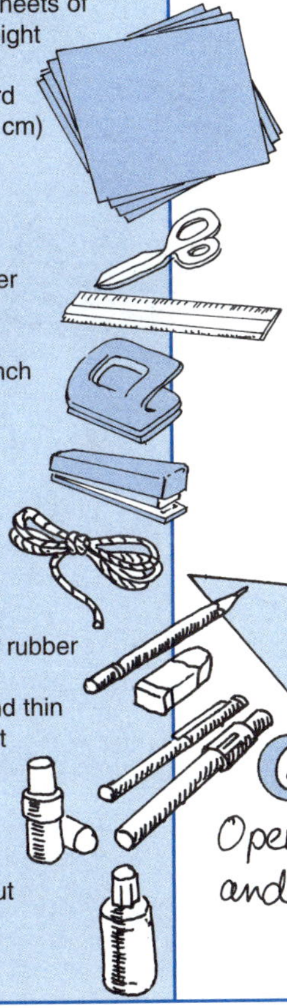

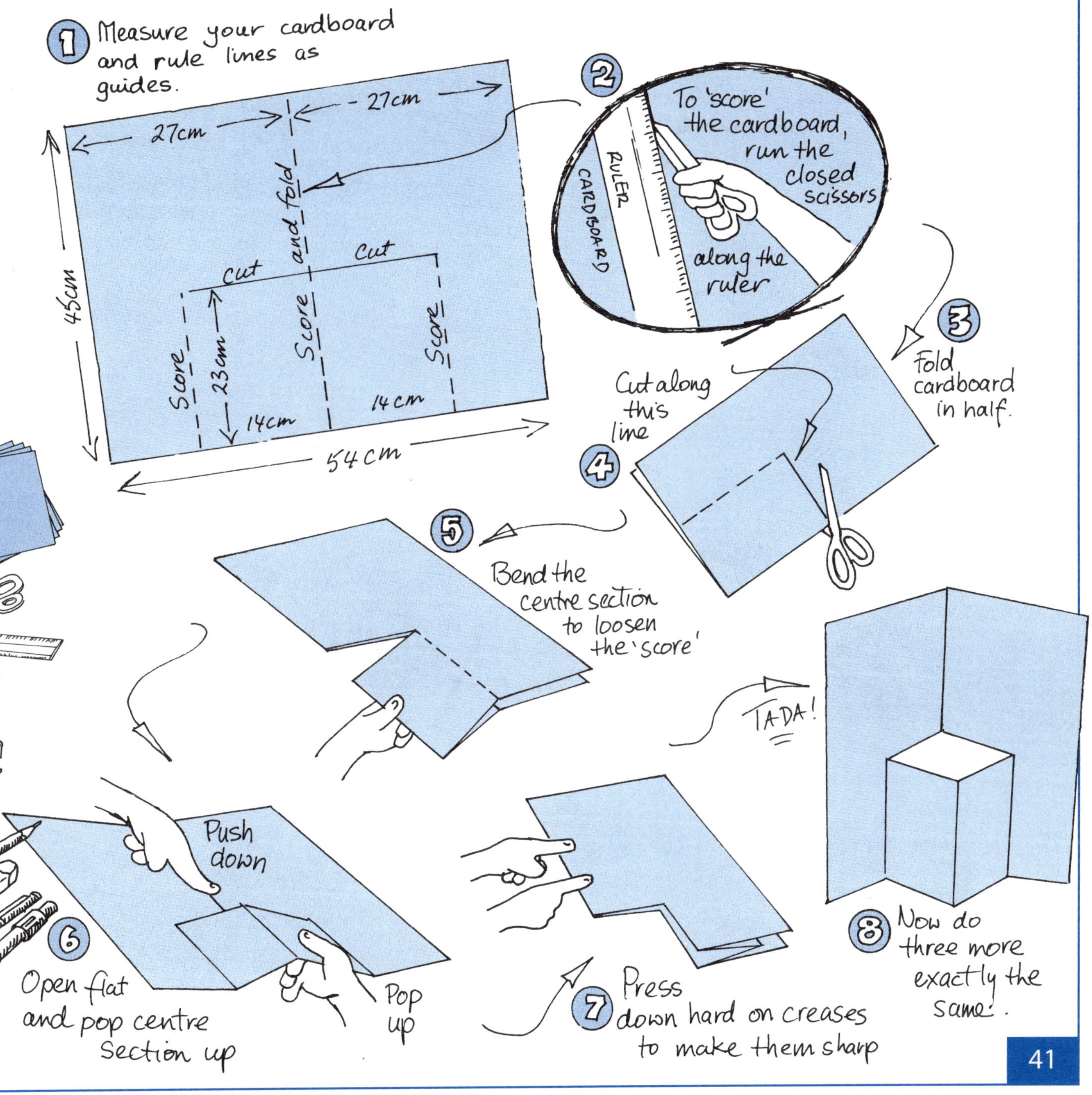

FRUIT SHOP MOBILE

9 Place two sections together and staple around the edge

10 Punch holes along the top edge (only use the centre holes)

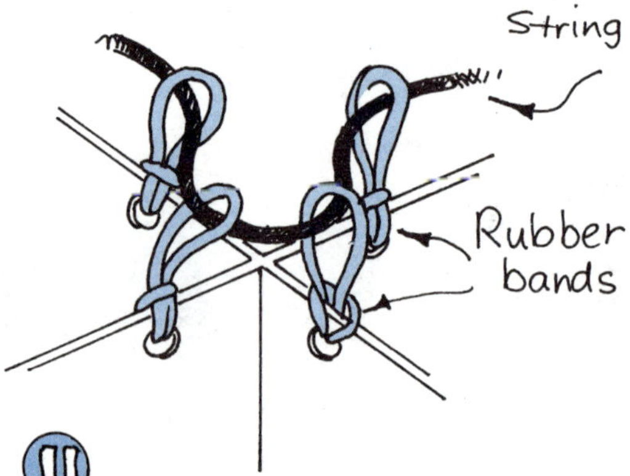

11 Place 4 rubberbands through the holes.

Thread string through the bands.

12 Decorate your mobile!

Cut and paste your 'decorations', or paint them on.

ADS FOR NEWSPAPERS AND SHOP WINDOWS

Design an interesting ad for your cubby, bike, garage sale, or anything you need to sell. Place it in the local newspaper (for a fee) or ask a local shopkeeper to stick it in their window.

YOU'LL NEED . . .

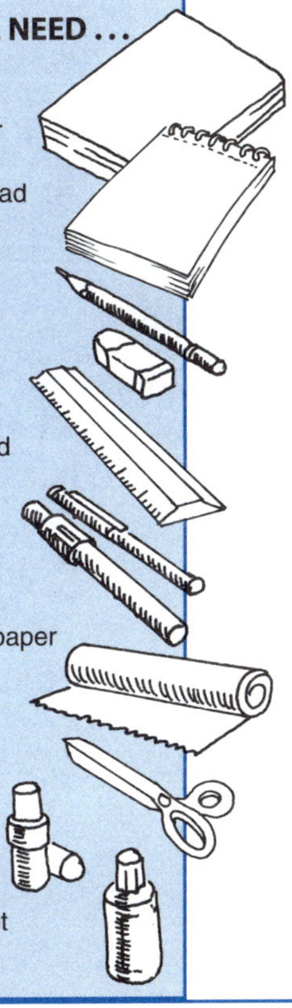

A4 paper

Sketch pad

Pencil & rubber

Ruler

Thick and thin black felt tip pens

Tracing paper

Scissors

Glue

White out

Three different designs for the same cubby.

Three different designs for a bike ad.

Two alternatives for a garage poster ad.

FOR SALE
PRE-LOVED
CUBBY HOUSE
$200.00 ono.
Phone (00) 1234567
NEW SWIMMING CENTRE FOR RYDE.
FOR SALE
YET ANOTHER NEW PRINCIPAL FOR SCHOOL
FOR SALE
Shop window
FOR SALE
or street pole

1. Do a rough layout so that you'll know how everything will fit, and how it will look.

2. Using the layout as a guide, rule a rectangular box on your good paper. This will be your 'Finished Art'.

3. Trace the letters on page 61. Follow the instructions for tracing on pages 6 and 7.

4. Draw a picture of your product. Try to make it an accurate copy, and keep it to the size allowed in your layout.
When finished, go over the pencil lines with a fine black marker.

5. Using a computer, type the details of your ad. Use 'bullets' to make the lines look like a list. Remember how much room you have for this text. You might need to adjust the size of the type so that it fits. Now, print it out.

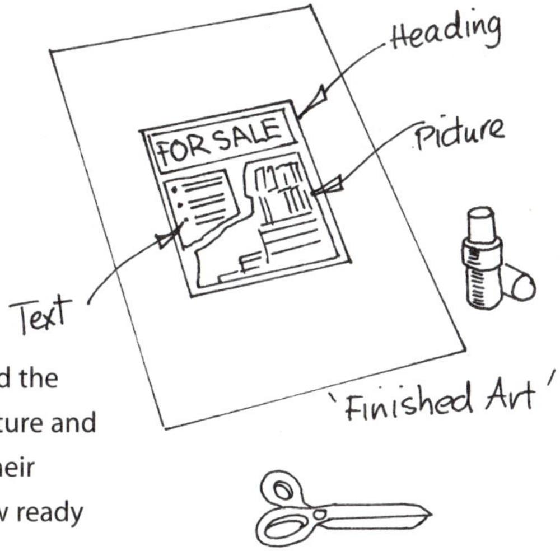

6. Carefully cut around the heading, text and picture and stick them down in their places. Your ad is now ready for printing.

SCHOOL FETE NEWSPAPER AD

Photocopy this template, fill in the gaps and you have a quick newspaper ad.

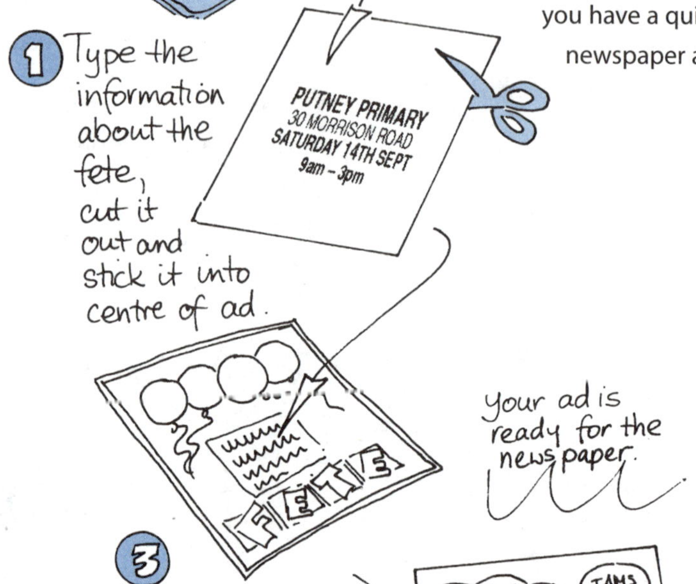

GREETING CARDS & STATIONERY

It's wonderful to receive a hand-made greeting card.
And when you turn it over to see the details on the back … a logo!

DEAR ______________________________

BE AFRAID
BE VERY AFRAID

DATE______________________

PLACE______________________

____

____

TIME______________________

COME DRESSED TO KILL!!!

OPEN INVITE OUT, TEAR ALONG DOTTED LINE, FASTEN WITH TAPE, POST BACK NOW, OR ELSE.

TEAR OFF AND SEND BACK!

☐ OK, I'm game

☐ NO WAY, HOZAY!

Name:______________________________

SO, you want a different sort of party? No probs! Just draw your own picture and stick it over the monster before photocopying. (Also, white out that 'afraid' stuff inside and replace with your own words.)

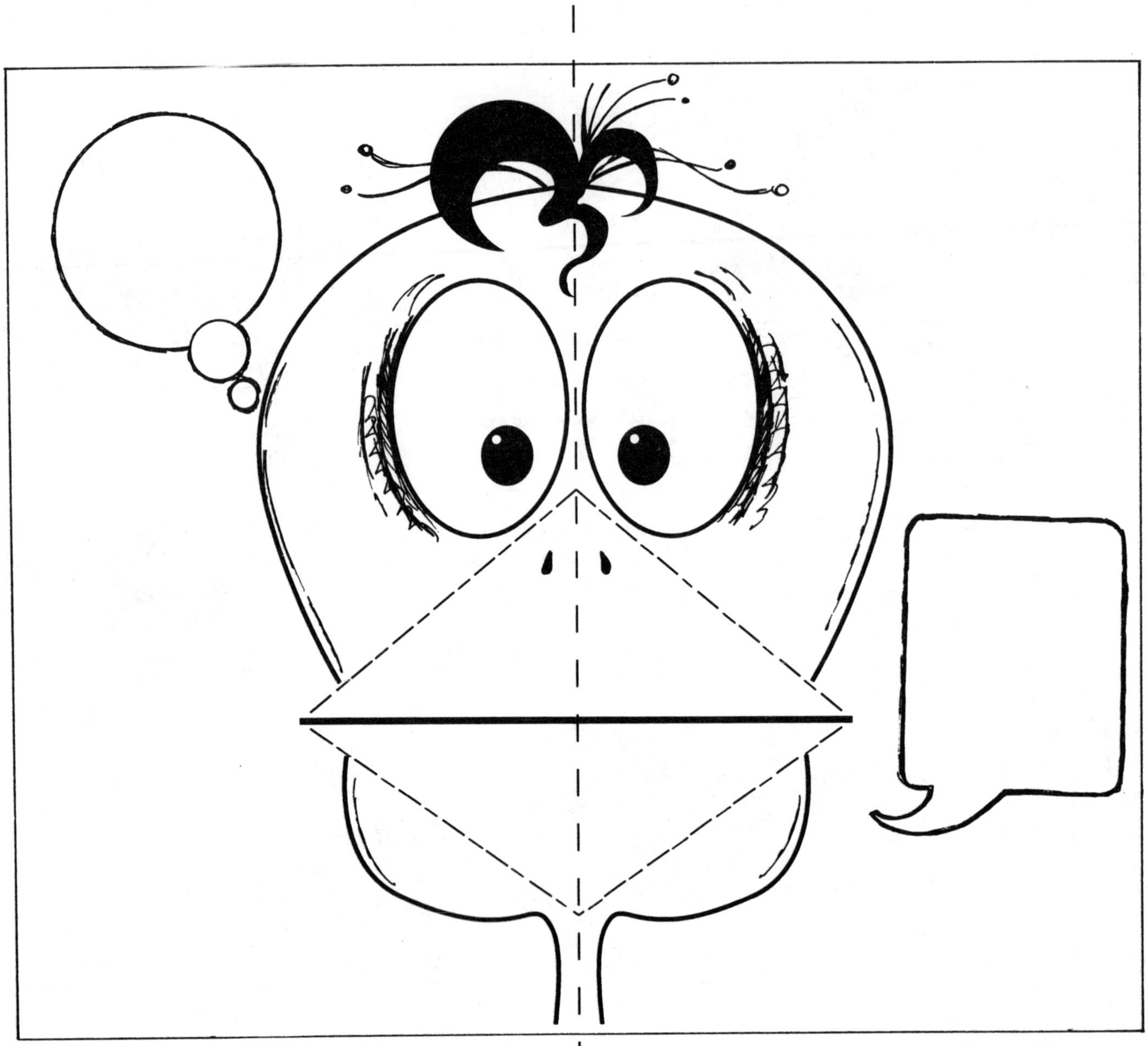

HELLO...

TWEET

GET WELL SOON

HAPPY BIRTHDAY !

BYE BYE

HOORAY !

Use one of these messages, or make up your own.

Cut out message, and stick it inside the speech balloon.

POP-OUT CANARY CARD

This greeting card can say anything you like. Write your message in the speech and/or thought bubbles. The outside of the card is blank while the inside has a pop-out fold that moves and appears to say the words. You can photocopy the template to save time.

YOU'LL NEED ...

Two sheets of coloured paper

Pencil & rubber

Black felt tip pens

Ruler

Tracing paper

Scissors

Glue

MASK PARTY INVITATION

1. Take an A4 piece of cardboard and fold it in half.

2. Trace the mask party art onto the front of the card and decorate with paint, ribbons, feathers and confetti.

3. Trace the mask template onto the inside of the card.

4. Handletter your greeting onto the back. Add instructions such as:
Cut out and decorate your mask. Fabulous prizes for most inventive and imaginative efforts!

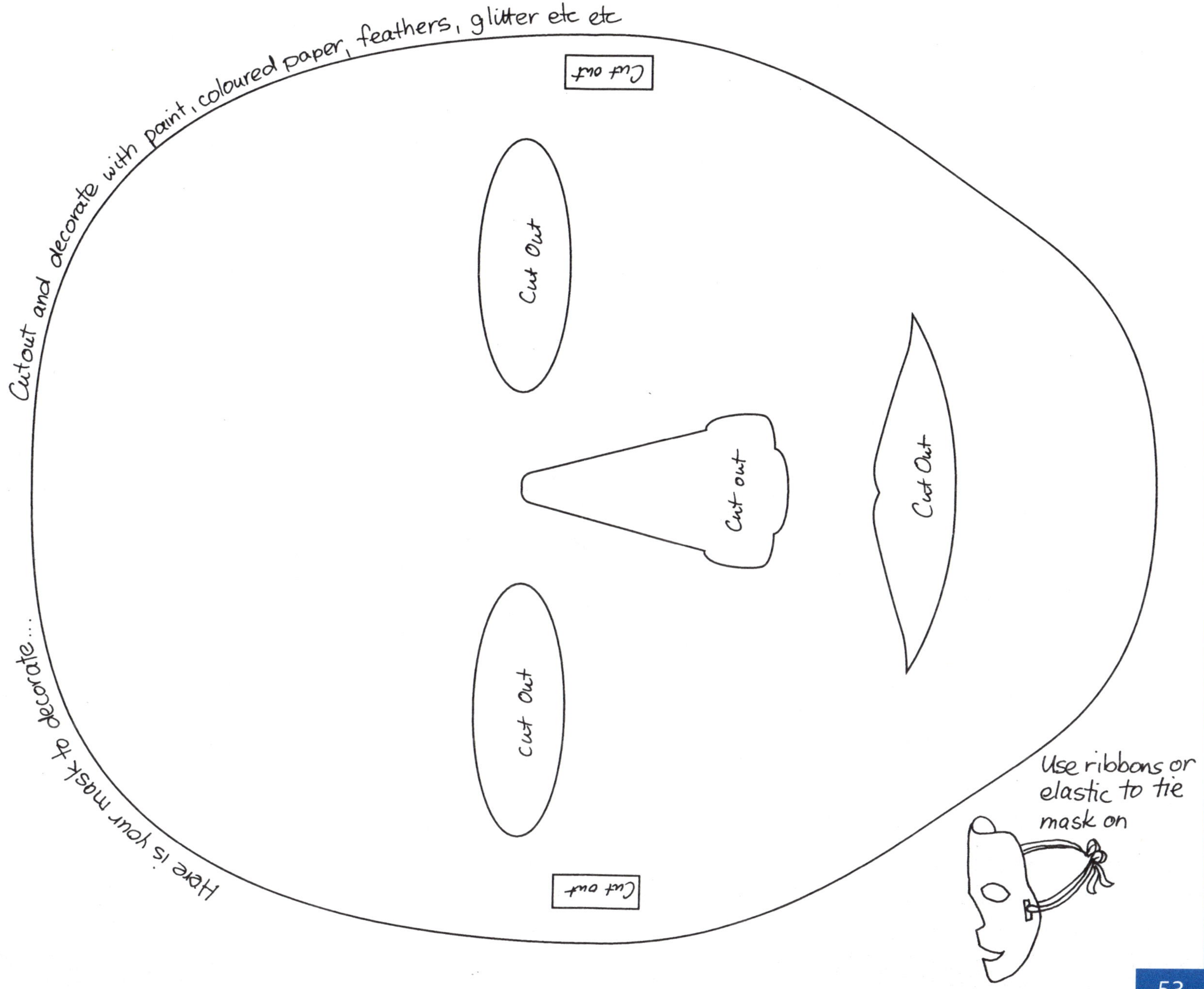
Cutout and decorate with paint, coloured paper, feathers, glitter etc etc
Cut out
Cut Out
Cut out
Cut Out
Cut Out
Cut out
Here is your mask to decorate...
Use ribbons or elastic to tie mask on

SLEEP-OVER PARTY INVITE

This design shows how different styles of lettering can look just as good as illustration. There are two sheets of paper in this invitation, and they need to be glued carefully along the fold.

YOU'LL NEED . . .

- Two sheets of white paper
- Pencil & rubber
- Black felt tip pens
- Ruler
- Tracing paper
- Scissors
- Glue

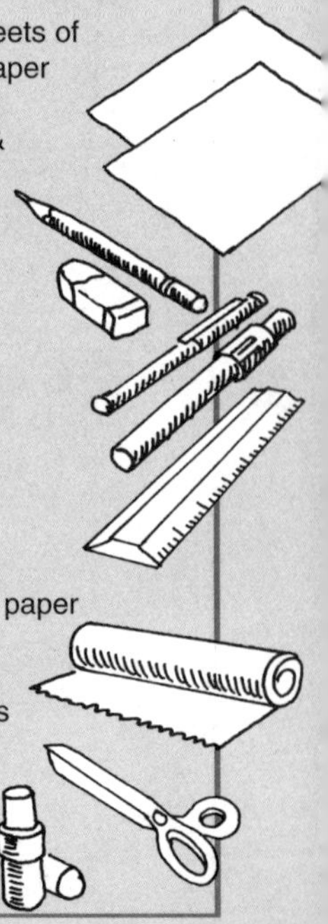

1 Start with two A4 sheets of white paper

2 Fold in half lengthwise

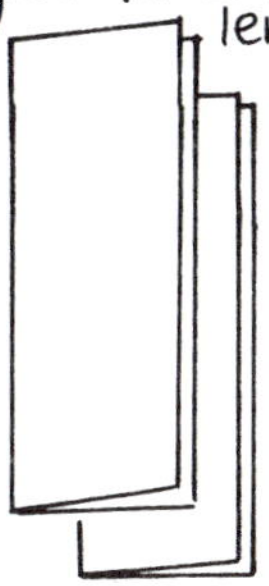

3 Cut off 9cm from each

4 Open out flat and do your artwork on the right section of each page.

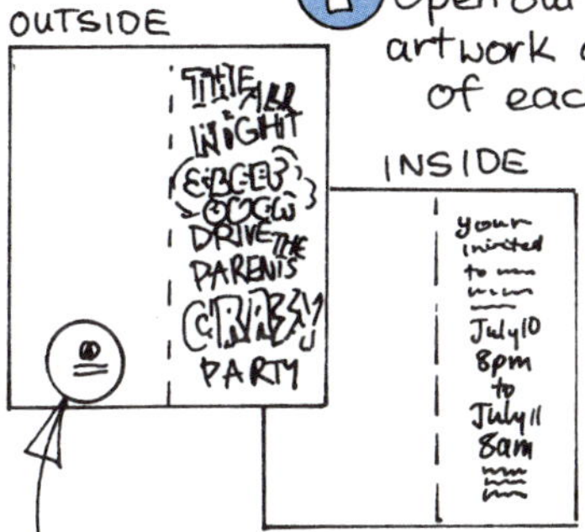

- The outside is the front cover.
- The inside has your details like time and date etc.

Do your own logo and draw it on the back of the 1st sheet

If you're little, get a big person to help

5 Decide how many invites you need.

- Check the spelling!
- Now photocopy your artwork onto coloured paper.
- The inside can be on white paper

6

Fold the outside sheets of paper in half

Fold the inside sheets of paper in half

7

Using glue or paste on the fold area only, slip the inside into the outside

Glue to go here only.

8 Now you only need to trim your cards back to the smaller size

Keep these offcuts – great for gift tags.

9 Your invitation will fit into a DL size envelope (business style)

PAINT YOUR OWN CARDS

Anyone can paint simple patterns like these. The trick is having the right shaped brush. It should be fat, round, and taper down to a point when wet.

Mix the paint with water so that it is sloppy, not sticky. Do some trial strokes on spare paper first, then paint on the card.

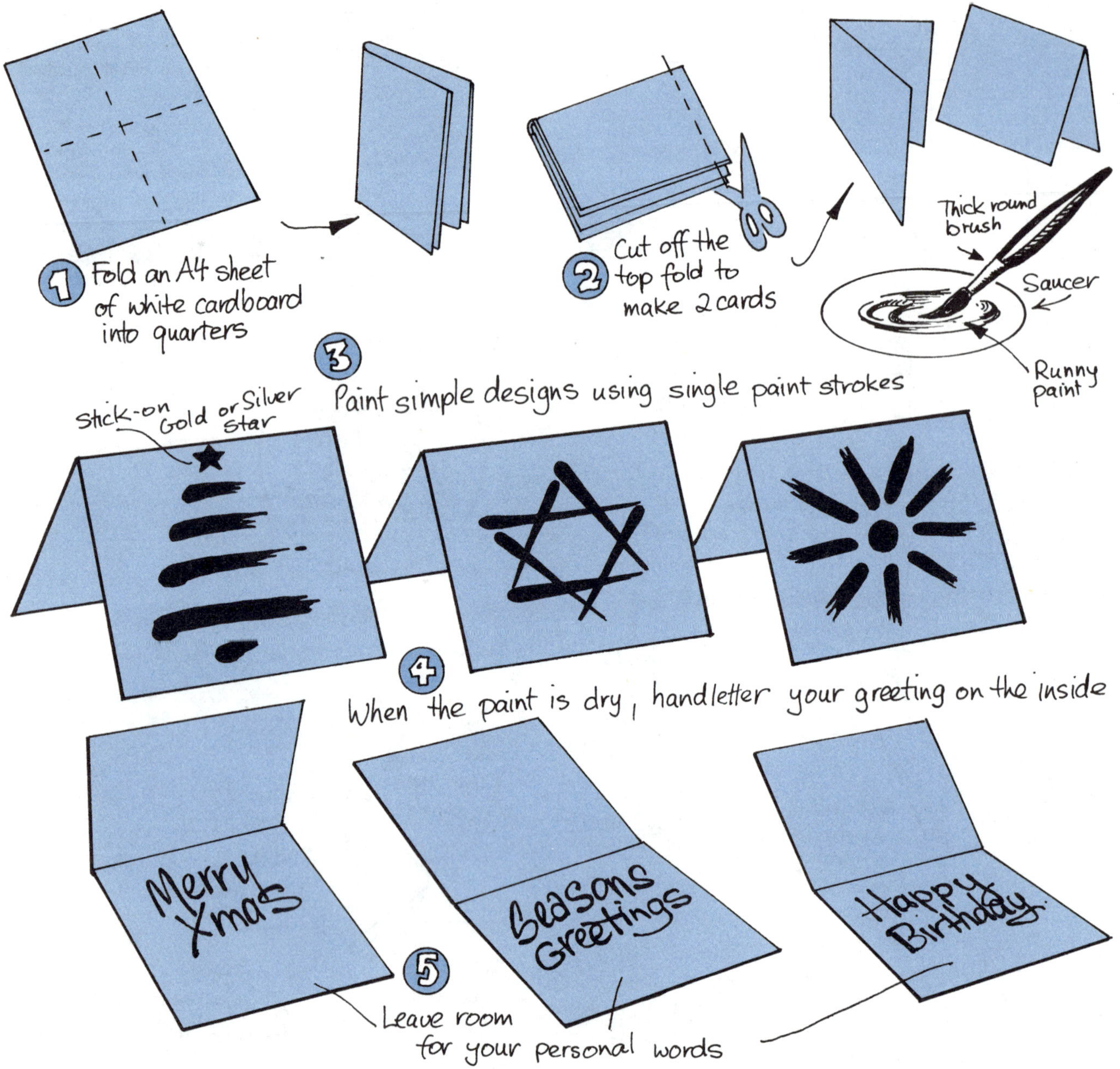

YOU'LL NEED . . .

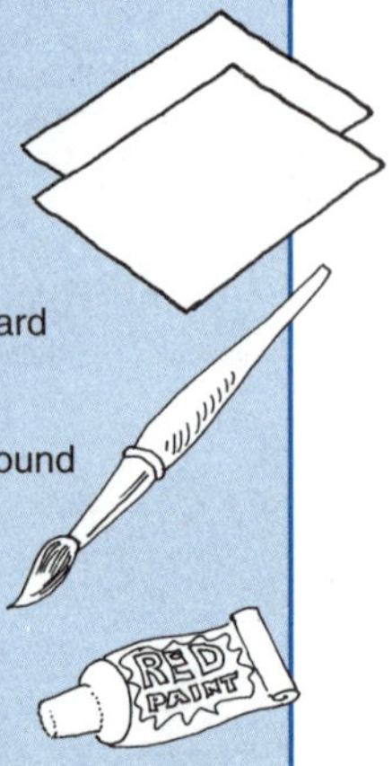

Lots of A4 cardboard

Thick round brush

Paint

STENCIL YOUR OWN CARDS

Make a stencil by cutting a simple shape out of cardboard.

Brush the paint from the outer edge to the centre so that it doesn't seep under the stencil and make a mess.

Fewer strokes look best, especially if they are a little bit transparent.

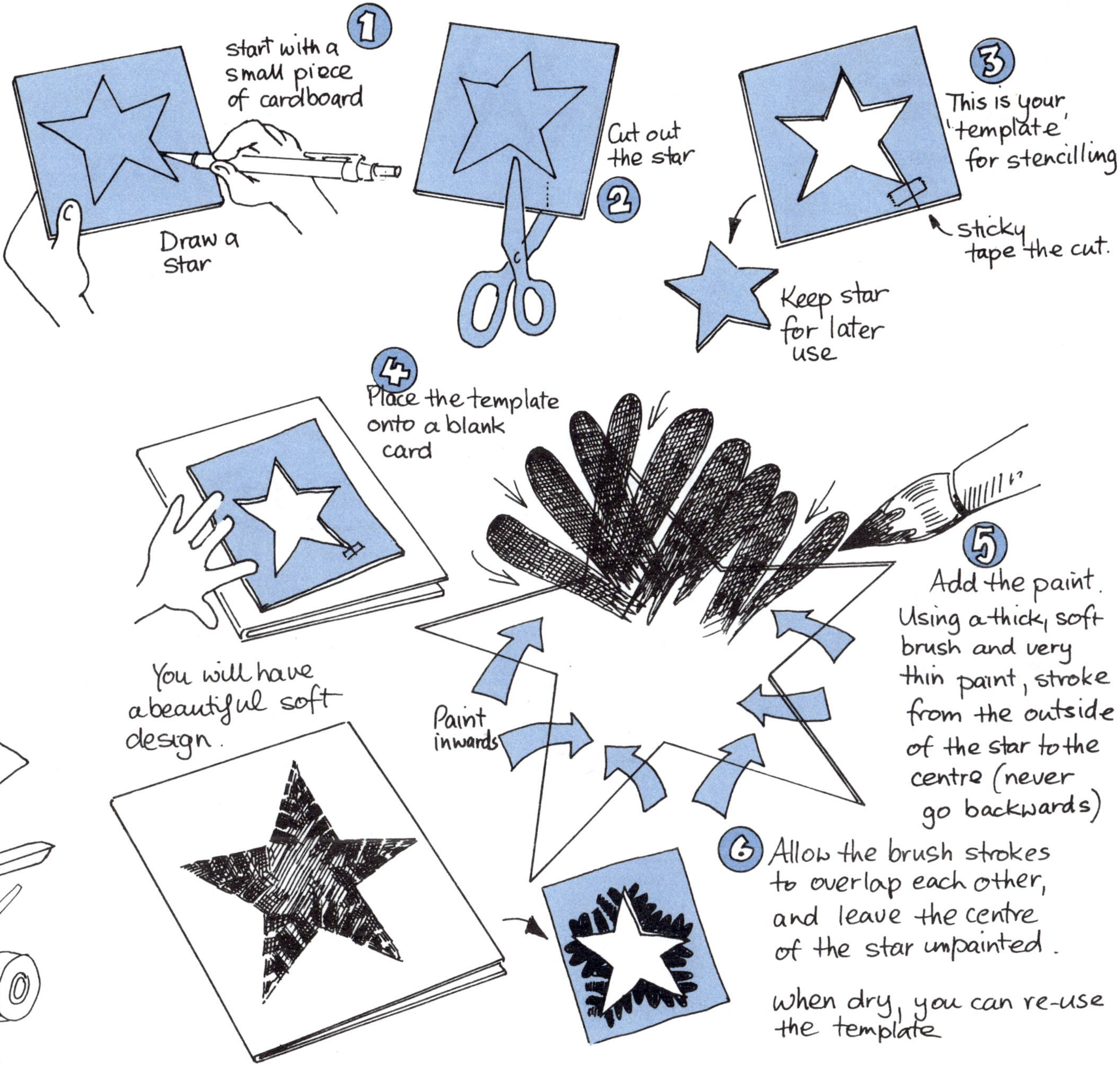

YOU'LL NEED ...

- Lots of A4 cardboard
- Scissors
- Thick round brush
- Sticky tape
- Paint

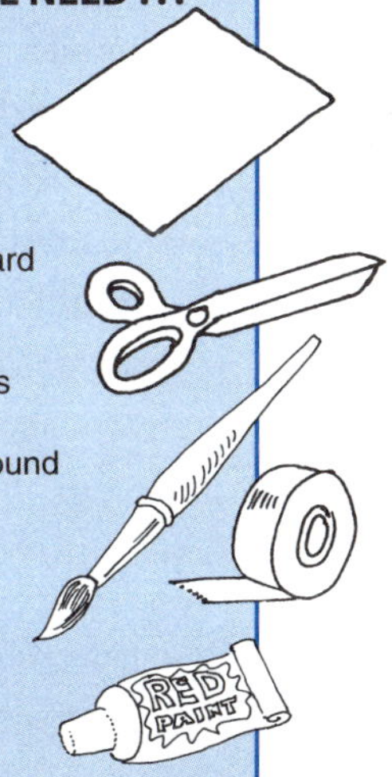

DESIGN YOUR OWN LOGO

A logo is a design that symbolises you and what you do. It can be based on your initials, your name, your hobby or sport, even your nickname. Put it on the back of your artwork. It works like a signature or a 'tag'.

If you have access to a scanner, scan it into your computer so that it can be used on your letterhead and other computer-based artwork.

Name
If you join the letters in your name, or your initials, together you create a 'log-of-type', which was where the term 'logo' came from.

Nickname
Your nickname can become a 'symbol' that is used as a logo.

Sport
Maybe you are passionate about a sport.

Your pet
A favourite animal can become a logo or symbol.

Any name
You can think up a new business name. Obviously, this one is 'Star'.

MAKE COPIES OF YOUR LOGO

After designing and drawing your logo, five photocopies at your school or library will give you 16 different sizes to use on artwork.

1. Decide on how your logo will look. Will you choose your initials, your name or a symbol?

2. Make a pencil sketch of your idea.

3. Refine your idea by drawing it again, then draw over it using a black felt tip pen and ruler.

4. Using a photocopier reduce the logo in size so that it is very small—about 2 or 3 cm high. Make two copies.

5. Cut out the second copy and stick it next to the first.

6. Photocopy this at 100% then stick these next to the first two. White out any 'shadows' formed by the cut edges of paper.

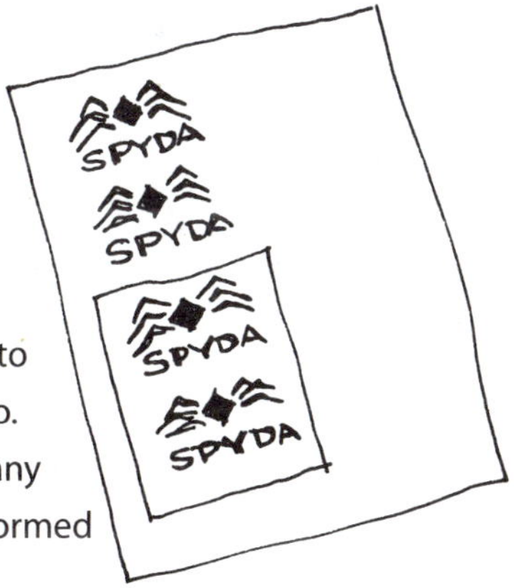

7. Set the photocopier to 60% reduction (this means that the copies will be 40% smaller) and copy the page. Stick the smaller copies next to the larger originals.

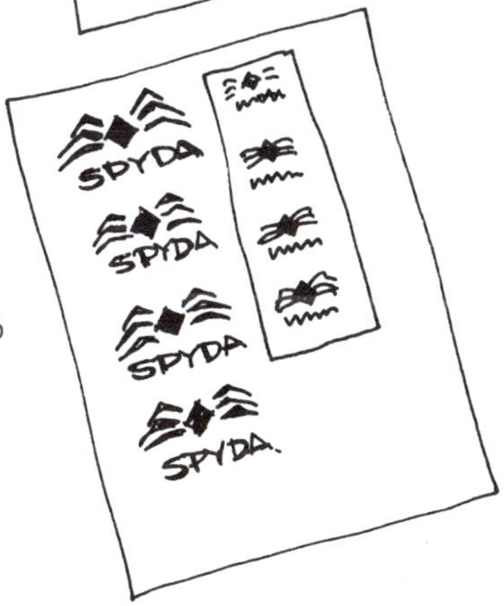

8. Keep the photocopier at 60% reduction and copy once more. Cut these out and stick them onto the master page. You will now have 16 versions of your logo.

YOU'LL NEED . . .

- A4 sheets of white paper
- Pencil & rubber
- Thin black felt tip pen
- Ruler
- Sticky tape
- White out

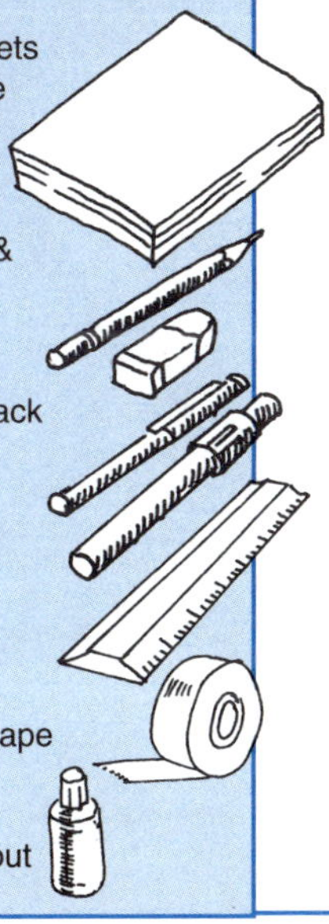

LETTERING STYLES

You can trace the letters as they are, or enlarge them to suit your layout. Enlarging can be done by this 'grid' method, or by a photocopier, where 100% equals same size and 200% is twice as big.

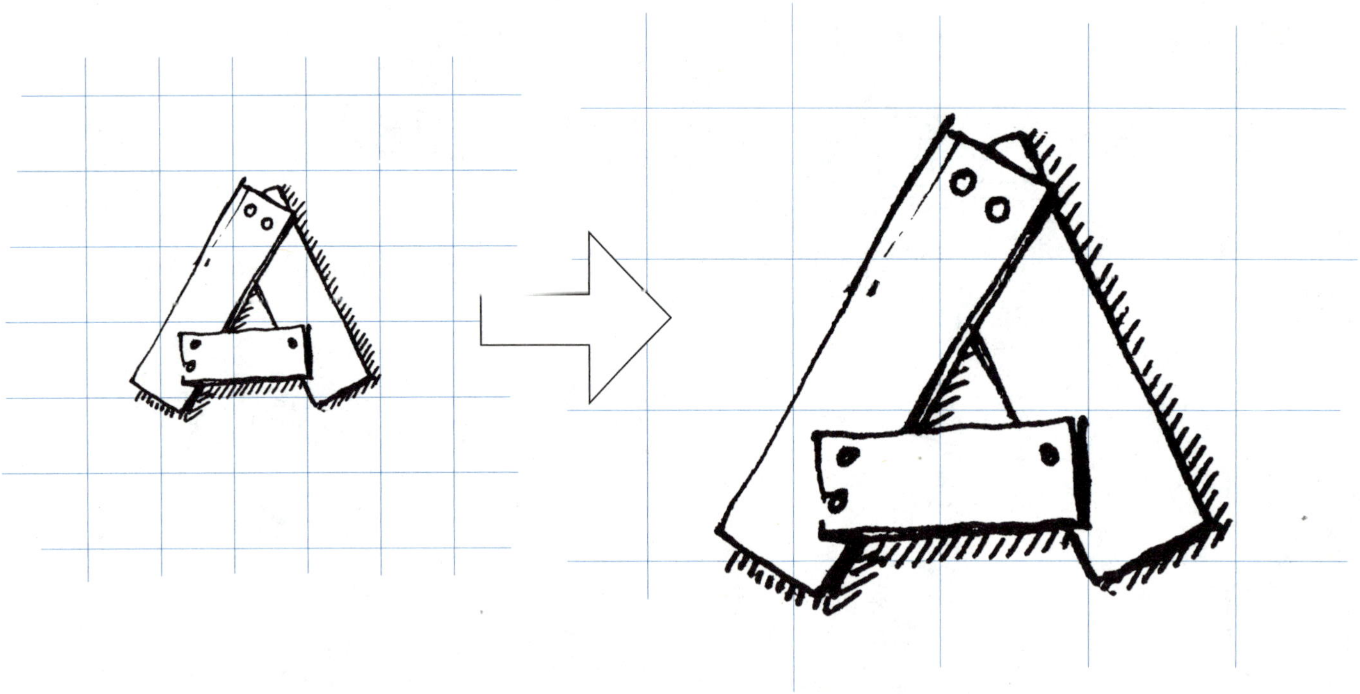

To enlarge letters and illustrations use the grid that is printed in blue, or draw your own grid lightly over an original drawing or letter. Next, make a larger grid for your new copy. Transfer the contents of each box into the larger grid.

ABCDEFGHIJ
KLMNOPQRS
TUVWXYZ
ABCDEFGHIJ
KLMNOPQRS
TUVWXYZ

ABCDEFG
HiJKLMN
OPQRST
UVWXYZ

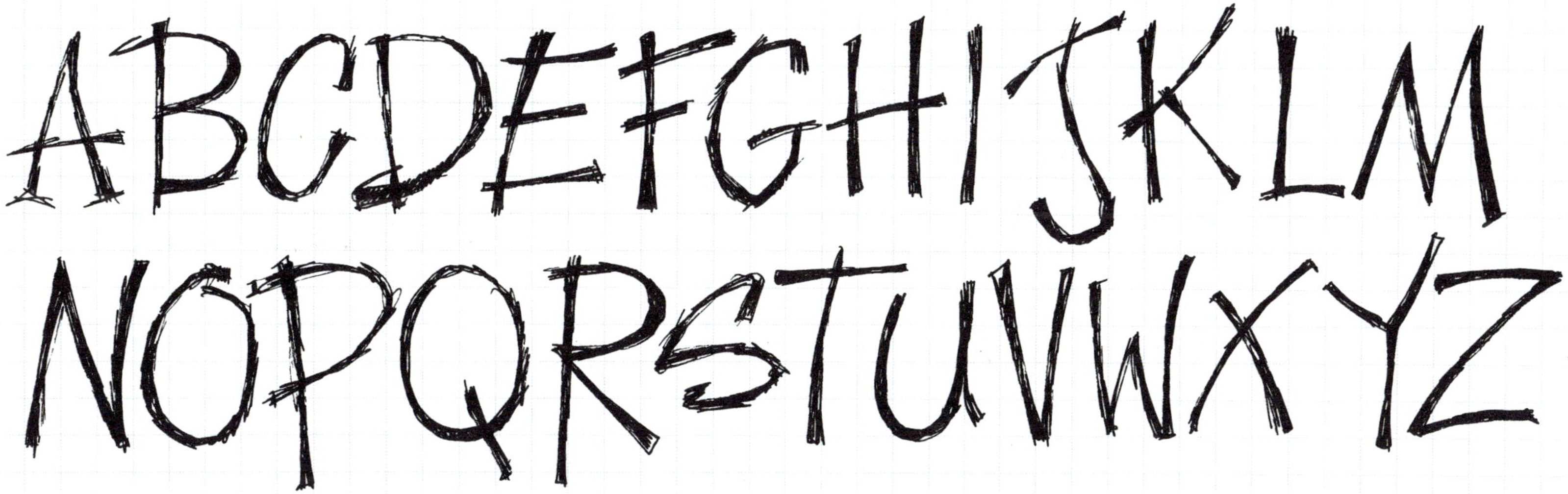
ABCDEFGHIJKLM
NOPQRSTUVWXYZ

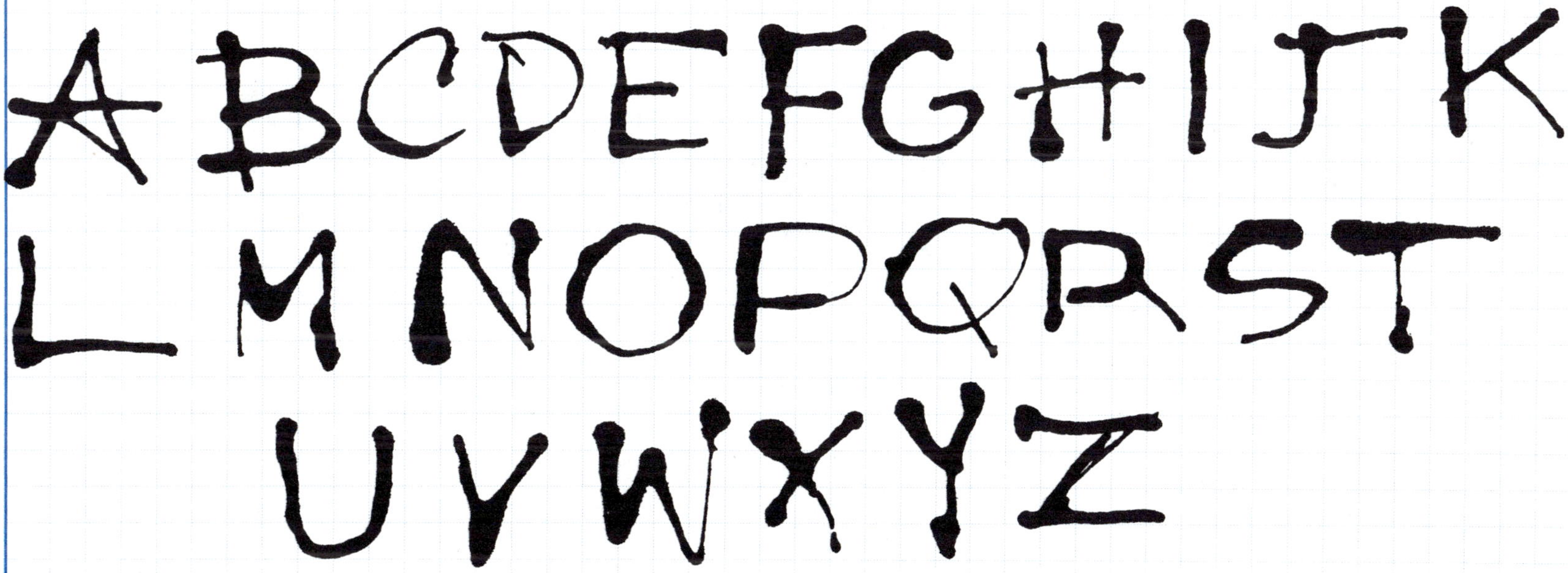
ABCDEFGHIJK
LMNOPQRST
UVWXYZ

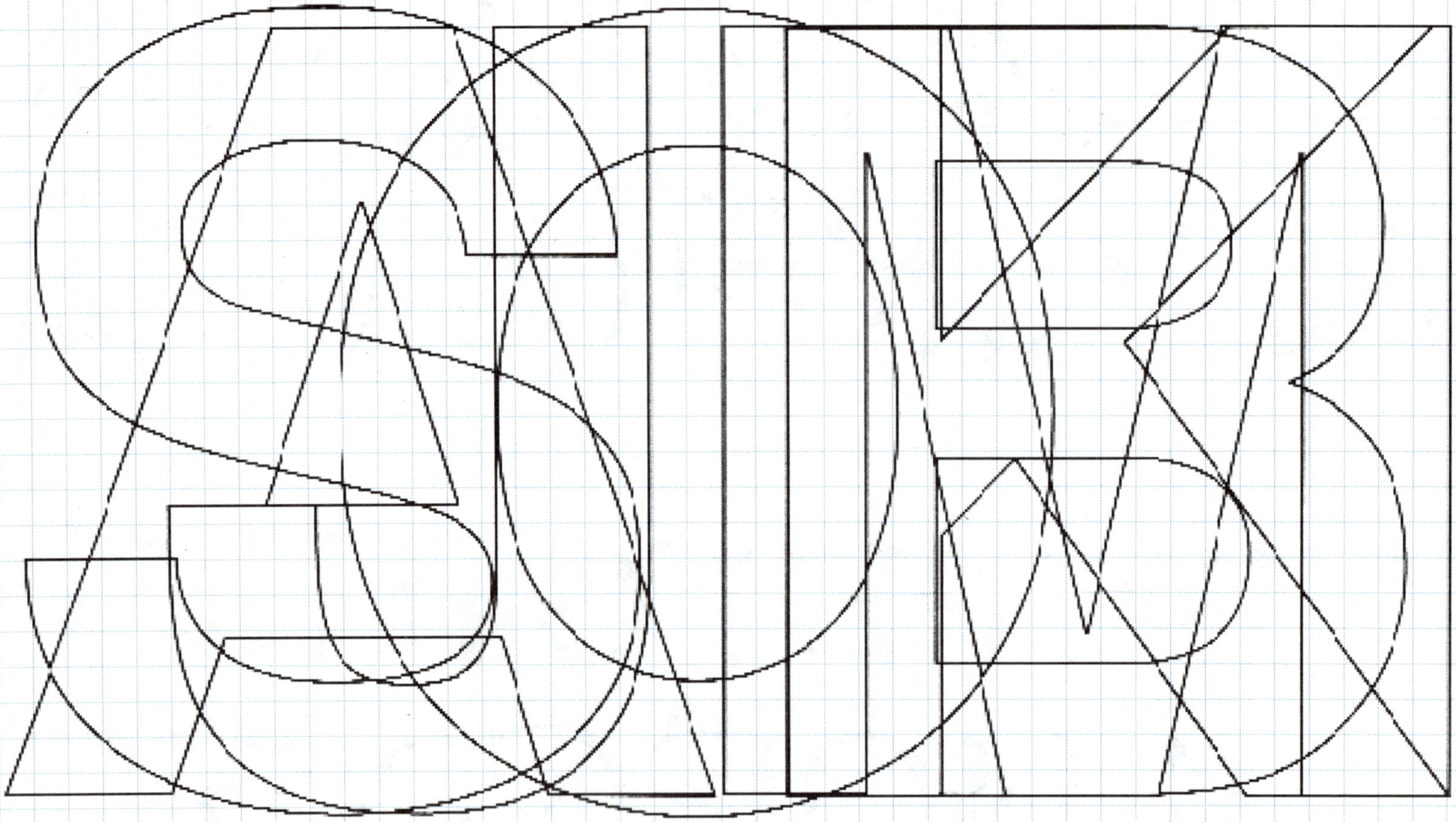

Wow! What a mess! Look carefully at these overlapping letters and you will see an A B O J K S and M. You can create just about any letter from these basic shapes. Use tracing paper and draw sections of your letter. You will need to mix and match these sections to create the letters that you need.

Good luck!